What's Great About ... I-95

MAINE TO FLORIDA

Interstate 95 is 1925 miles long.

The traveler who wants to make the most of the trip finally has a
tool to make the journey as enjoyable as the destination.

The secret is knowing what makes that section of the country unique.

The goal is to enrich your journey.

INTERESTING INTERSTATES
www.interestinginterstates.com

HOW TO USE THIS BOOK

Each spread, or double page, shows a range of mileposts (MP) at the top of the page. There is an average of 30 miles between spreads.

•

Usually the mileposts line up with exit numbers but some states have kept sequential exit numbering. In that case, the body of the text usually helps to mark the subject's location.

•

Many spreads refer to both mileposts and exit numbers to help you locate an item of interest.

•

Maps are provided as general guides, not for exact navigation.

•

Placement of an item on a map is approximate and used only as a reference to suggest the location.

•

Every effort has been made to provide accurate and timely information. The writers, researchers and publisher cannot be held responsible for errors or omissions.

•

Driving south, read front to back.
Driving north, read back to front.

•

Drivers, please keep your eyes on the road.
Rely on a navigator to read about the entries.

•

Enjoy your journey.

Opal Publishing Company
2167 Ferguson Road
Allison Park, PA 15101

ISBN-13: 978-0-9824538-2-7
ISBN-10: 0-9824538-2-5

Table of Contents

Smyrna

(1)

(2)

Houlton

95

Katahdin

(3)

Millinocket

Howland

(4)

Twombly

(5)

Old Town

Sebasticook Lake

Skowhegan

(7)

(6)

Bangor

Mexico

(8)

Augusta

Bar Harbor

South Paris

Lewiston

(9)

295

Freeport

Portland

(10)

Old Orchard Beach

Kennebunk

Kennebunkport

Kittery (11)

Portsmouth, NH

95

MAINE

307 MILE

Rush hour at the US/Canadian border at Houlton.

In 2006, 704,268 passenger vehicles crossed through at Houlton.

This last bit of interstate before the Canadian border bears the distinction of the least traveled road in the interstate system. It's also the easternmost piece of the interstate puzzle.

HOULTON'S LITTLE AMBASSADOR

In 1982 a little girl from Houlton worried about talk of nuclear war. To ease her concerns, ten-year old Samantha Smith wrote a letter to the Soviet Premier Yuri Andropov asking if he intended to start a war.

Then the unexpected happened.

He sent a personal reply not only assuring her of his peaceful intentions but also extending an invitation to her and her family to visit his country. Samantha accepted his invitation, spending two weeks in the USSR.

They loved her.

America's Youngest Ambassador, as she was called, was honored by the Soviets with a dahlia, a tulip, a concerto, an asteroid and even an ocean vessel named in her honor.

Tragedy struck two years after her visit when she died in an airplane crash. She's buried in Houlton.

Maine remembers her every first Monday of June; that's officially Samantha Smith Day.

Samantha Smith commemorative stamp issued in the USSR.

POST 291

Typical traffic at the US/Mexico border near Tijuana.

At the Mexico crossing in 2006, 17,135,163 passenger cars drove through.

Interstate 5 in Southern California carries
one of the nation's heaviest traffic loads.

Picture from Creative Commons/Wadester16 at Wikipedia

SMYRNA

The little town of Smyrna at Exit 291 holds a surprise. In 1996
a few Amish moved here in search of relief from the press of
civilization. Weary of the ever-prying eyes of tourists, they found
solitude here in Smyrna. Hard working and honest, they are
welcomed by the townsfolk.

The Meduxnekeag, a small creek that crosses I-95 near the border, has appeared on maps and journals since at least 1793 but it seems it's never spelled the same way twice. From Meduxnakic to Madishnakick or stretched to Meductinicikick, it's no wonder locals call it simply "The Creek."

AROOSTOOK COUNTY - THINK POTATOES

Near MP 260 you cross the southern border of the largest county
this side of the Mississippi River.
You can call it Aroostook but locals just say "The County."

After dominating the country's potato production in the early 20th
century, competition from western states and Canada has eaten
away at the county's slice of the potato production pie.
Despite that, more potatoes are grown here than anywhere else.

SCHOOL'S OUT!

Like a blast back to 1750 when Scotch-Irish farmers introduced
potatoes to Maine, school kids still get a three-week break in
September and October to help with the harvest. It's a break from
brainpower but not muscle power. These kids work hard even though
now most harvesting is done by machine.

NOW THE POTATO INDUSTRY IS DIVERSIFYING.

Scientist have figured out how to convert potatoes into plastics.
Products we rely on every day such as water bottles and carpeting
can now be made from potatoes instead of crude oil. Unlike corn, this
advancement will not rob us of a food source; potato peels and other
waste may be all that's necessary to make enough plastic.

Watch out for these two when you get out of the car, especially May through July when they are most active.	
No-see-ums are so small you hardly know they are there until your skin stings from their bite.	While the male Black Fly politely feeds on nectar, the female likes to add a little blood to her diet at your expense.

POST 255

The scenic overlook at MP 255 (northbound only) offers your only view of Katahdin, barely seen here lurking in the morning mist. Maine's tallest mountain is hidden by trees along the interstate.

MOOSWA

Native Algonquian Indians referred to the enormous animal munching on birch and willow shoots (as well as pond weeds and grasses) as mooswa, or "twig eater."

Their long, gangly legs are perfectly adapted for wading through either ponds or drifts of snow. Those heavy antlers, up to six feet across, drop off before winter sets in to conserve the bull's energy. They sprout again in the spring and take three to five months to grow back.

ATTENTION

NEXT 6 MI

Be on the lookout - you don't want to tangle with a bull moose, which can weight 1,500 pounds and stand seven feet at the shoulder. Studies show the most common conditions for a moose collision are June through December in dry weather at night when darkness hinders evasive action.

Paper has been manufactured in Maine for over 270 years, but it didn't start with trees.

The MILL in Millinocket doesn't refer to the paper mill. The name means "dotted with many islands." in the local Indian language.

Back in the 1700's paper was made from rags – discarded clothes.

It wasn't until the rag shortage in the 1850's that paper producers thought to use wood pulp.

LOGS WAITING TO TURN INTO TELEPHONE BOOKS IN EAST MILLINOCKET

TODAY'S PAPER COMPANY

Katahdin Paper Company now runs the mill in Millinocket, but recently the challenges of the papermaking business are overwhelming.

Rising fuel costs have forced the company to temporarily shut down but they are fighting back. The best weapon is in their own back yard.

Bark.

Biomass generators, which burn bark instead of oil, save substantially on fuel costs. Renewable forests provide pulp to produce paper and also the energy to get it done.

Katahdin in Baxter State Park
The first step southbound on the Appalachian Trail.

The Appalachian Trail starts (or ends) at the summit of 5,267-foot Katahdin, Maine's highest peak. Adventurers hiking the Trail immediately face the One Hundred Mile Wilderness. Signs warn to pack food for seven to ten days because you are completely on your own – no mini-marts to grab a Coke and some jerky.

> Katahdin means "Greatest Mountain" in the Abenaki language - so saying "Mount Katahdin" is redundant.

WHICH CAME FIRST, THE MILL OR THE TOWN?

In the late 1800's an engineer recognized the falls on the Penobscot River were ideal for generating power for a pulp and paper mill. When the Great Northern Paper Company started business here in 1900 it was the largest paper mill in the world. But there was no town near the mill.

Millinocket was created to support the paper company.

WOULDN'T WE ALL WANT OUR POLITICIANS TO FOLLOW THIS LEAD?

Great Northern once owned most of the land in this vicinity. When hard times hit the paper industry soon after the stock market crash of 1929, Great Northern sold some of its holdings to Percival Baxter, governor of Maine from 1921 to 1925. He bought 6,000 acres including the great mountain, Katahdin, for $25,000 and turned right around and donated it to the state with the condition it would always remain wild. He continued to buy more land to donate to the state but his greatest gift was yet to come. He left a seven million dollar trust to manage the land so it would never burden taxpayers.

Summer's greens yield to autumn's riot of colors.

When nighttime temperatures sag into the 30s and the sun warms the daylight hours, those sugar maples and birch trees respond with a spectacular jewel-toned display.

Looking for the perfect view?

Maine's rangers have been tracking the progress of leaf color and leaf fall for fifty years. In season, look for a weekly update on www.mainefoliage.com.

Nature's Bounty Doesn't End There.

One of Maine's major cash crops is blueberries, the kind that grows wild. They love the nutrient-poor soil left by the glaciers 15,000 years ago.

Maine produces 99% of the wild blueberries in the United States and most grow in Washington County 70 miles to the west. Here in Penobscot County berries contribute $75 million to the economy.

Even though they are wild and don't need to be planted every year, there's still work to be done. For instance, every May a billion bees are imported to pollinate the blueberry flowers.

POST 201

Alton Bog near Howland at MP 201

Bald Eagles and other uncommon birds, plants and animals, enjoy the marshy meadow of Alton Bog.
Stand on the carpet of the bog and you'll feel the moist squish of peat holding water trapped by a clay floor.

THERE'S NEW YORK CITY AND THEN THERE'S TWOMBLY

You may wonder, driving through these dense woods, "Does anyone live around here?" Mainers are notorious for requiring plenty of space to spread out. Many regard a neighbor living five miles away too close for comfort.

Take Twombly, for instance.

The 2000 U.S. Census noted that a married couple, age 68, were the town's only residents. Twombly, 20 miles east of Howland and in the middle of nowhere, was one of only five places in the U.S. with two residents.

Quoting from Wikipedia, an online encyclopedia, "There are 11 housing units (apparently 10 are empty)."

But time changes everything. The 2010 Census updated Twombly's status: it now has a population of zero.

The Penobscot Nation and Old Town at Exit 197

Around 1775, the English, keen on acquiring land for the king, negotiated deals with trusting Penobscot Indians. Little by little, the Indians' land was whittled away and, by 1820 when Maine became a state, the tribal land was reduced to an island in the middle of the Penobscot River. The English called it Old Indian Town.

Old Indian Town became simply Old Town. Then, during the area's restructuring in 1840 even the name Old Town was taken from the tribe and applied to a new, white settlement on the other side of the river. The island nation's land was then known as Indian Island.

The Penobscot National Seal

A hundred and fifty years later the tribe sued the American government and won. Big. In 1980 the tribe, many of whom still live on Indian Island, were awarded 150,000 acres of land and $81.5 million dollars in restitution.

Baseball's Cleveland Indians official website uses the words "supreme baseball talent" and "a marvel" to describe Louis Sockalexis, the Penobscot man who played for the team from 1897 through 1899. Back then the team was known as the Cleveland Spiders but was often nicknamed "the Indians" because of their Native American player. To enhance their image in time for the 1915 season, the team name was changed to the Cleveland Indians, reviving the old nickname referring to the talented Penobscot player.

POST 184

If shivers run down your spine near MP 184, the cause might be Mt. Pleasant Cemetery, right next to the interstate. Just a few miles from Stephen King's house, it could have inspired some of his horror novels.

Bangor's King family is an active and vital part of the community.

Steven and his wife, Tabitha, took those creepy stories that kept many of us hiding under the covers and turned them into something remarkable for thousands of budding athletes.

The Shawn T. Mansfield Stadium, a baseball stadium dedicated to a boy who tragically died at a young age, was possible only through a $1.5 million donation from the King Foundation. The state-of-the-art stadium is well used, even hosting the Senior Little League World Series.

At about MP 185 glance down at the Kenduskeag Stream as you cross over. You might see a kayaker running the rapids. This stream, whose name means "eel catching place," comes alive in April during the annual Kenduskeag Canoe Race.

Games (in season of course) can be heard live on WZON (620 AM), a sports radio station owned by Mr. King.

Or try his other station WKIT (100.3 FM) as you drive along the interstate.

BANGOR

In the 19th century it was a bold claim to call your town "the lumber capital of the world" but, with 700 seafaring boats moored in Bangor's lumber port on a typical day, the claim was true.

Lumber was shipped all over the world from Bangor; some vessels rounded South America's Cape Horn en route to California to help the 49'ers, fortune seekers headed west for gold. Towns sprung up overnight but there wasn't enough prepared lumber for all the construction. Many wild west saloons, jails, sluices and corrals were built with wood shipped in from Bangor.

I-95 crosses over Sebasticook River at about Milepost 151. Not far from there the river meets Sebasticook Lake and that's where the story starts.

There is a mysterious ancient contraption hiding in the lake.

You can't see it from the road. In fact, you can't see it even if you're standing on the shore.

Sebasticook Lake, shown here with a low water table, is near Exit 157.

It was a coincidence that anyone even found out it was there.

When they found it, they didn't know what it was.

Here's the story:

1992 was a very dry year. Lake levels were so low people noticed something in Sebasticook Lake they'd never seen before; several odd wooden stakes jutted out above the surface. Very unusual. It took a scientist to determine what it was – perhaps the oldest existing fish weir in North America.

This is a more modern weir in Canada.

Carbon dating showed portions of the rig were nearly 6,000 years old. Ancient man, far older than those who built the Pyramids in Egypt, built a fish trap at the mouth of this lake, where fish siphoned in from the river. Subsequent generations of this tribe added to and modified the fish trap, or weir, but after four thousand years or so they abandoned the production.

Trapping fish in weirs was a sophisticated concept considering that man was just discovering how to cultivate food at that point in history.

The era is called the Late Archaic-Early Woodland period and predates Stonehenge by 2,000 years.

Mmmm - Maple Syrup

You can make it yourself if you want. Next February, put on warm boots and wade through the snow to find a sugar maple that's at least ten inches around (measured 4 ½ feet from the ground). Drill a hole two-inches deep and tap a spout into place. Hang your bucket and wait for six weeks. If you're lucky enough to get ten gallons of watery sap, boil it down and bottle up your syrup – a whole quart of it.

Or, instead of all that work, you can go to a local farm to get your supply. Look for that proud "Maine Maple Syrup" label, the only sure sign it was tapped and processed in Maine.

Commercial sugarcamps, particularly in northern Maine, tap tens of thousands of trees. But instead of traipsing out into the field to tend to buckets, they attach tubes to the spouts, miles of it in some cases. Sap runs straight from the trees into the sugarhouses.

Tapping trees properly doesn't do them any harm. In fact, some of the best-producing Maples are over a hundred years old.

134 MILE

BENEDICT ARNOLD was a pharmacist, bookseller and a war hero but most of us know him as a traitor.

Before his act of treason, Arnold lead a thousand men up Maine's Kennebec River in support of the colonists' invasion of Canada during the Revolutionary War. The Quebec Expedition didn't go in Arnold's favor – he retreated in defeat.

That was in 1775, five years before he was caught in a plot to hand West Point over to the British.

On the island where Benedict and his men made camp is a place called Arnold Park. A lead canteen left behind after their encampment is now in the local museum. The 300-year-old white pines on the island are officially recognized by the National Register of Historic Trees since they were "witnesses" to that bit of history.

ICE HARVESTING

When you cross over the Kennebec River at about MP 134 you'll see that the name, which means "long, quiet waters," is a good description.

Because the waters are mostly calm, it can freeze solid in the dead of winter. In 1814, long before air conditioning, Fredric Tudor knew how hot and muggy southern summers could be. "The Ice King," as he was known, cut the ice into large blocks and stored them in icehouses until the change of seasons. When Southern Belles sweltered in the summer heat, Mr. Tudor delivered ice to cool them off - for a profit.

At the height of his career, India was his most lucrative market despite the four-month boat trip.

POST ME 95 133

About 13 miles north of Exit 134 is the quiet town of Skowhegan.
Sometimes even quiet towns have something to crow about.

Skowhegan does.

The Skowhegan State Fair is the nation's oldest agricultural fair.
When it started in 1818, it was the only way for otherwise remote
families to share tips about better farming and homemaking.

But they had a lot of fun too.
Harness racing is one 19th century activity that's still popular today.
Hoochy-koochy shows were all the rage too.

Today the fair is more popular than ever;
over 7,000 exhibitors and performers show up every August.

No kidding, Skowhegan's jail
was for sale in 2008 – listed as a
multi-family dwelling.

Can you name the first woman to run for president?

It was Victoria Woodhull, who ran in
1872 on the Equal Rights Party platform.
But Skowhegan's Margaret Chase
Smith, shown here, was the first woman
nominated by a major political party.

She didn't get the presidential nod but
served Maine in Washington D.C. for 32
years as both a U.S. Representative and
U.S. Senator.

Augusta, Maine's Capital City

From the perspective of I-95, Augusta might not seem like the best location for a thriving community, much less the capital of Maine. To the contrary, its situation on the Kennebec River made it a perfect place to settle.

The Red Paint People, named for the red iron oxide found in their grave sites, must have agreed. There is evidence that they camped here 4,000 years ago. Although these expert deep-sea fishermen preferred to live by the shore, they traveled the forty miles from the ocean up the Kennebec River to hunt bear, moose and deer near here.

Why stop here? The same reason future generations of settlers stopped here; this is the headwaters of the Kennebec; navigation farther upstream required smaller boats and more effort.

Virginia's Jamestown Colony is known as the new world's first permanent settlement. Maine's Popham Colony, established just a few months later, hardly gets a mention in history books.

The group from England, led by George Popham, tried to establish a town at the mouth of the Kennebec in 1607. Although the colony lasted little more than one year, they managed to accomplish at least two noteworthy things.

1. They explored upriver, to the place of the future Augusta, gathering valuable information to send back to England.

2. In one year they built a 30-ton ocean-worthy vessel named Virginia, which they used to sail back to England.

This sketch is from their original map now stored at the Archivo General de Simancas, the Spanish archives.

POST 109

OLD FORT WESTERN

In 1754, Fort Western was built here near the shore of the Kennebec River.

Yes, it was a military fort built in a strategic location that allowed the British to assert influence over the colonies.

But that, in the history of America's oldest wooden fort, is not its most enduring role. After all, it served as a fort for only 12 years.

Captain James Howard, one of the fort's original occupants, didn't leave when the military moved out. Instead, he bought the property and turned it into a trading post selling everything the aspiring settler needed, from sewing aids to rum. For fifty years his family catered to the needs of their neighbors.

After years of neglect, a local publisher rescued the fort in 1922 and turned it over to the city of Augusta, which made it into a museum demonstrating the variety of Maine life in the 18th century.

MAINE'S STATE TREE AND FLOWER

This part makes sense: the tallest tree in eastern North America, the Eastern White Pine, is Maine's official state tree.

This part makes you scratch your head: Maine's official "flower" is the Eastern White Pine's tassel and cone. It's the only state whose flower isn't a flower.

LEWISTON

You might not expect this, but Lewiston is very international. The double attraction of mill jobs and a train connection between this city and Canada brought many French-Canadians to the area in the 1800's. They stayed and today provide the base for a rich Franco-American culture.

FARMERS' ALMANAC

Since 1818 the Farmers' Almanac has been a household name, especially around farming communities. Not to be confused with the Old Farmer's Almanac started 26 years earlier, this periodical is published in Lewiston, Maine. Readers enjoy tips on gardening, cooking, fishing and even when to find the best fall foliage but it all got started with weather predictions. The secret formula for calling weather trends up to two years in advance relies on sun spots, tidal action and astrological positioning.

M E
95

TOURMALINE, MAINE'S STATE ROCK

Elijah and Ezekiel, taking a shortcut home in 1820, caught a flash of green in the dirt near Paris, Maine. They had discovered a vein of tourmaline. The location, Mount Mica, turned into America's first gemstone mine. Mount Mica is still giving up gifts of small green and red crystals like the one pictured here.

Just where is Mount Mica? Although the exit for South Paris is at Exit 63, the mine is about 20 miles northwest of MP 80, near Paris. Paris is north of Poland, which is southeast of Sweden and Norway. Peru and Mexico are farther north.

As you pass the Lewiston Sports Complex at Exit 80 think of Ali and Liston.

Boxing champion Sonny Liston took on Cassius Clay in a Miami Beach boxing ring on February 25, 1964. It stunned the crowd when Liston didn't get off his stool to fight in the seventh round. Clay won by a technical knockout. The next day he announced to the world from then on he would be known as Muhammad Ali.

Why does that matter here in Maine?

Ali two years after the Lewiston fight.

After that surprising end to the Miami fight, a rematch was ordered, but this time Sonny Liston was the challenger. The second match was staged before 2,434 fans in Lewiston, Maine on May 25, 1965. It was by far the smallest crowd for a championship match. Liston was flat on the mat before the end of the first round.

OLD ORCHARD BEACH

When Thomas Rogers settled here 350 years ago, he planted fruit trees and grape vines on high ground facing Saco Bay. Sailors could see the plantation from their ships. The well-known landmark began to appear on maps and was named Old Orchard Beach, now OOB for short.

Who needs a runway anyway?

In the early years of aviation, level fields usually served as runways. But OOB had something even better: a seven-mile packed sand beach. As long as the tide was out, it was perfect for take-off.

Charles Lindbergh brought the Spirit of St. Louis here unexpectedly. His scheduled stop, Portland, was socked in with fog so he landed on Old Orchard Beach instead.

Trivia:

Was Charles Lindbergh the first pilot to fly across the Atlantic Ocean? No, over 90 pilots made the trip before him. So why did he turn into such a celebrity? Two reasons: he was the first solo flyer and he landed in Paris, full of cheering fans and lots of press taking pictures of the new hero.

OOB's Palace Playland, New England's only beachside amusement park, is especially busy on balmy Thursday evenings when families gather on beach blankets to watch their fireworks.

Kennebunk's Lafayette Elm

Years after France's General Lafayette aided America in her fight for independence, President James Monroe invited him to visit the U.S.

Lafayette addressed a crowd in Kennebunk, standing beside a fledgling elm tree, which was honored with the name Lafayette Elm.

This stately specimen, measuring 131 feet tall and 17 feet around in 1920, became the town's symbol. Dutch elm disease ravaged the tree in the 1960's and now a plaque stands where Lafayette delivered his speech.

In neighboring Kennebunkport,
the Bush Estate
is clearly visible from the public beach.

George Herbert Walker, a wealthy banker and a leader in the local Democratic Party, built a grand house in 1903 on a spit of land jutting into the sea. His daughter Dorothy married a Bush and together they purchased daddy's estate, then known as the Walker Compound.

Their son, George Herbert Walker Bush, the first Bush president, spent many of his younger years here and inherited the estate.

His son, George Walker Bush, the second Bush president, visited the family estate on summer vacations and entertained heads of state such as France's Nicholas Sarkozy and Russia's Vladimir Putin.

The Piscataqua River Bridge sweeps across the river between New Hampshire and Maine.

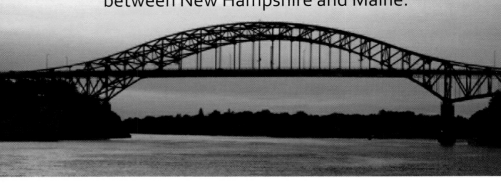

Kittery, the oldest incorporated town in Maine, guards the mouth of the Piscataqua River and Fort McClary guarded Kittery.

The Old Block House at Fort McClary is now a museum.

Can you imagine a U.S. vice-president cooking for the troops?

Here's a little-known historical fact: Abraham Lincoln's first vice-president Hannibal Hamlin (who had also served as Maine's governor) enlisted in the Coast Guard during the Civil War and served as a cook at Fort McClary.

Even before the Portsmouth Naval Shipyard was established in 1800, this harbor was the site of important milestones in shipbuilding.

For instance, the British commissioned their first warship built in the New World here in 1690.

Then the *Raleigh*, built here in 1776, became the first ship to go to battle flying the American flag and is now the focus of New Hampshire's state seal. Some say *Raleigh*'s sister ship *Ranger* was first to fly the Stars and Stripes.

Both states tried to claim the islands in the Piscataqua where the shipyard is located. It wasn't until a U.S. Supreme Court decision in 2001 that everyone knew for sure that the Portsmouth Naval Shipyard was in Maine. Portsmouth is still in New Hampshire.

The Portsmouth Naval Shipyard's mission these days is refurbishing nuclear-powered submarines.

A mile south of the Maine / New Hampshire border

There are no signs mentioning the former Pease Air Force Base immediately west of I-95 in NH, but as one of NASA's launch-abort and emergency landing sites, until the shuttle program shut down in 2011, there was a miniscule chance a space shuttle could roar overhead on its way to touch down there about a mile from the interstate.

Portsmouth

①

NEW HAMPSHIRE

Seabrook

② Newburyport

95

MASSACHUSETTS

③ Danvers

Salem

Concord

④ Lexington

⭐ Boston

90

Norfolk

⑤ Braintree

Plymouth

44

Pawtucket

Providence ⑥

195

Hope

95

⑦

RHODE ISLAND

(1)	MP 4-1 in New Hampshire Seabrook, NH		Pages 30-31
(2)	MP 86-85 in Massachusetts Newburyport, MA		Pages 32-33
(3)	MP 66 Danvers and Salem Village, MA		Pages 34-35
(4)	MP 46-45 Lexington and Concord, MA		Pages 36-37
(5)	MP 32-26 Norfolk and Plymouth, MA		Pages 38-39
(6)	MP 42-36 in Rhode Island Providence, RI		Pages 40-41
(7)	MP 19-7 Hope, RI		Pages 42-43

Voting technology has changed since this contraption was used over a hundred years ago.

Every four years we hear about the "New Hampshire primary" over and over again on the news. Traditionally New Hampshire holds the nation's first presidential primary election, a position that other states envy. So New Hampshire is in a race of its own: the vote, originally scheduled for March, has inched to January 8, chased by other states who want to be first. As an additional weapon, other states are crying, "Not fair!" They say New Hampshire, ranked 42nd in population, doesn't necessarily reflect the pulse of the nation in general and, therefore, shouldn't have a lock on the first-in-the-nation primary.

BOOZE AND GAMBLING RIGHT ON THE INTERSTATE.
MIND YOUR SIN-TAX!

Liquor stores and lottery outlets might be unusual at an interstate rest stop but that's one way New Hampshire makes up for having no sales tax or income tax. It must be working because, although their property taxes are among the highest in the nation, overall taxes are among the lowest.

Seabrook Station Nuclear Power Plant

You can't see it behind the trees along the road but Seabrook Station Nuclear Power Plant, with the largest nuclear reactor in New England, is a stone's throw east of the interstate near MP 1.

It churns out enough electricity to fuel 900,000 homes and also welcomes visitors to its Science Center featuring Chilly Willy, the rare blue lobster. The Owascoag Nature Trail, an elevated boardwalk winding through woods and marshland, is another environmental addition to the facility.

Brightest after shedding an old shell, the blue lobster nearly glows with an azure hue.

One of these beauties comes along, well - once in a blue moon. They occur in nature at a rate of about one in two million.
Chilly Willy isn't the only one in captivity.
The one pictured here lives at the Audubon Society of Rhode Island in Bristol.

Look for the Purple Heart Trail signs near both ends of New Hampshire's 15-mile section of I-95.

George Washington initiated the idea to honor those who fought for our country and were wounded at the hands of our enemies. In recognition of their service, Washington gave them the Badge of Military Merit – now called the Purple Heart. The Purple Heart Trail is a state-by-state effort to further acknowledge their sacrifices. Starting in Mount Vernon, VA, Washington's home, the Purple Heart Trail spreads throughout the U.S. into 45 states.

The name Harriet Spofford may not stand toe to toe with other Massachusetts' literati like Longfellow and Nathaniel Hawthorne, but she was a best seller in the late 1800's pumping out Gothic tales and romantic yarns with heroic women characters.

If you're not into literature, you might like bridges. The 1792 span connecting Deer Island to the mainland is Chain Bridge, one of the country's oldest suspension bridges.

Crossing the Merrimack River at about MP 86, northbound traffic gets a good view of her house on Deer Island, where Harriet lived and died. Southbound traffic gets only a quick glimpse of the roof top.

THE NAVY BEAN BECAME MASSACHUSETTS' OFFICIAL STATE BEAN IN 1993.

What color are NAVY BEANS?
White.

Why are they called NAVY?
Sailors relied on these beans during long voyages.

Native Americans had a great recipe using beans, bear fat and maple syrup.

Mixed together in a deerskin and baked, it eventually turned into a luscious sweet concoction. Bostonians like the dish but, with a glut of molasses, they swapped that for maple syrup. Bear fat made way for salt pork. That's the history of Boston Baked Beans.

July is national bean month.

POST 85

While you hurry across northern Massachusetts, you are driving through a section of the country that spawned a new word.

Political misdoings are nothing new.

This 1812 political cartoon satirizes Massachusetts' Governor Gerry's re-apportioning certain electoral districts to affect the next election's outcome.

Gerry's convoluted district looked like a salamander to some people and the new monster took the name Gerry-Mander.

Gerrymandering is now part of our lexicon, defined as manipulating constitutional boundaries to gain political advantage.

TRIANGULAR TRADE
IT STARTED WITH RUM. OR DID IT START WITH SUGAR?

New England rum was considered the best in the 18th and 19th centuries. Newburyport was a major player in the rum game along with 62 other Massachusetts distilleries of record in 1763.

NEW ENGLAND
To make rum, distillers needed molasses and that came from the sugar cane fields in the West Indies.

AFRICA
Slave traders in West Africa gladly bought New England rum in exchange for slaves.

WEST INDIES
To raise the sugar cane, growers needed slaves to work the fields.

A 1876 depiction of a Salem Village witchcraft hearing.
The Puritan minister Cotton Mather wrote about evil witches.

The sign on the interstate tells you Exit 48 (near MP 66) is for Danvers but what it doesn't tell you is this: Danvers used to go by the name Salem Village.

Despite common thought that the 1692 witch hysteria centered in Salem, it started here, along the I-95 route.

The Salem witch trial stories are tantalizing and familiar but the bones of the story bear repeating. When two girls (cousins aged 9 and 12) fell ill, the village doctor determined the girls were bewitched. Pushed to finger the culprits, the girls pointed to (obviously innocent) neighbors. Twenty people were executed as witches; four more died in prison. Many of the 150 or so imprisoned "witches" lived nearby, practically on the path of today's I-95.

THE EPISODE LINGERED ON.

In 1709, after people got their heads on straight again, three convictions were overturned. Following another petition in 1711, 22 more were reversed. Two more victims were exonerated in 1712 and the matter was put to rest for about 250 years. Then in 1957 descendents of victims asked for their loved ones' names to be cleared but the proclamation named only Ann Pudeator and "certain others." It took another major push to get every individual who was accused of witchcraft in 1692-1693 recognition and exoneration. Finally in 2001, over 300 years later, it was done. The governor signed the proclamation clearing all accused on October 31 – Halloween.

> The people of Massachusetts identify so closely with Cape Cod Bay that, by official proclamation in 1990, they are to be called Bay Staters.

THERE IS NO SHORTAGE OF MASSACHUSETTS STATE SYMBOLS. THE COMMONWEALTH'S WEB SITE LISTS 54 OF THEM.

I-95 is never closer to the Bay than near MP 66 so it's the perfect place to mention a state symbol that is a giant of the sea - the Right Whale.

The name is sadly accurate: the Right Whale was the right whale to hunt - swims slowly, close to the surface. That's why it was hunted nearly to extinction in the 1700's and they are still in jeopardy. It is estimated that only 300 North Atlantic Right Whales exist today.

Other State Symbols

Norman Rockwell is the official artist. Dr. Seuss is the official children's author and illustrator.

ROOM FOR ONE MORE?

Herman Melville's masterpiece Moby Dick became the state's Epic Novel in 2008 thanks to a petition from Pittsfield's elementary school students.

THE REVOLUTIONARY WAR STARTED HERE

In the spring of 1775 tensions were high between the British soldiers and the colonists.

With an itchy feeling that the Brits might make a move, the sexton stood watch in the North Church.
According to plan, he would signal by lighting one lantern in the church steeple if the enemy approached over land. If they "went out by Water" then he'd light a second lantern.

When the threat was clear, Paul Revere and others thundered on horseback toward Concord to warn the colonial militia, men who were ready to fight for their country at a minute's notice.

Revere's ride, which ended in capture, took him directly across the path of today's Interstate 95 near Exit 30 (MP 46).

A National Historic Park commemorates the bloody clash between the Minute Men and British soldiers, a skirmish that started the eight-year Revolutionary War.

Brutal hand to hand combat occurred right here at Exit 30 and several British soldiers were wounded. They were treated, but died, at Ebenezer Fiske's house, whose foundation still exists just feet from I-95.

THERE'S A WEALTH OF HISTORY AT EXIT 29 NEAR MP 45

PAUL REVERE'S RIDE

It's hard to imagine a more symbolic memento of our nation's fight for independence than the lantern used in Boston's North Church to signal the British were coming. The Concord Museum displays that along with possessions of Ralph Waldo Emerson and Henry David Thoreau.

WALDEN POND

Between Concord and the interstate, about 5 miles from Exit 29, is Walden Pond where Henry David Thoreau spent two years of his life in a one-room cabin. The glacial kettle pond achieved nearly mythical status after he published introspective accounts of his observations and experiences.

ORCHARD HOUSE

Louisa May Alcott lived in Orchard House, situated nearby on the road to Concord, while weaving tales based on her family life. *Little Women* was an instant success and declared a classic almost as soon as it came off the press. A tour of the family's home gives insight into Louisa's inspiration.

Norfolk County

No signs along the interstate inform you that you've entered Norfolk County, the site of several historical events. There are too many to list.

One that's almost beyond coincidence is this:
four of our country's presidents were born in this county.

1797 - 1801	1825 - 1829	1961 - 1963	1989 - 1993

John Adams	John Quincy Adams	John F. Kennedy	George H. W. Bush

A WORLD-WIDE FIRST and ONLY

Just south of Exit 17 near MP 32, in the median strip and hidden behind rows of trees is something that is found nowhere else in the whole world. The Norfolk County House of Correction and Jail is the only detention facility located in the median strip of a major highway.

Not as honorable as the gentlemen pictured above, the two guys shown here still made a name for themselves. **Sacco and Vanzetti** were accused of the 1920 murder of two men in Braintree, seven miles directly east of the I-95/I-93 intersection near MP 26.

Held in the Norfolk County Jail (not the newer one in the median), their trial and subsequent execution ignited debates and bombings. Still controversial, discussions of their guilt and the fairness of their trial continue into the 21st century.

MAYFLOWER, THE SHIP AND THE PLANT

The trailing arbetus, or mayflower, is Massachusetts' official state flower. Although it grows throughout eastern North American, it has been on the endangered species list since 1925.

THE MAYFLOWER

Pilgrims came ashore aboard the Mayflower 30 miles east of MP 26 in the 1600's, establishing the Plymouth Colony and friendly relations with the native people.

The First Thanksgiving by Jean Leon Gerome Ferris depicts two cultures peacefully sharing the autumn bounty. The woman appears to be offering a helping of what came to be Massachusetts' state bird; the turkey.

PAWTUCKET

Pardon me, but that's AMBASSADOR Potato Head.

Yes, the top dog in the Potato family that was conceived by Hasbro, Inc. in Pawtucket in 1952 was chosen by the state as their Ambassador of Fun. After all, he has plenty of media experience having been the first toy advertised on television and then appearing as a principle character in the movie *Toy Story.*

G.I. Joe, also born in Pawtucket, is only a little jealous.

RHODE ISLAND'S RARE ROCK

Our nation's smallest state is home to a vein of Cumberlandite. This 1.5 billion-year-old slightly magnetized rock is found only in Rhode Island and so was named their state rock.

POST 36

The Rhode Island State House, home to the General Assembly and offices of the governor, rivals St. Peter's Basilica in Rome and the Taj Mahal. Only those two plus the Minnesota State Capitol have larger self-supporting marble domes.

PROVIDENCE

Going north, it's a stretch to get a good view of the State House near MP 38. Southbound traffic has a clear shot.

Independent Man, the bronze statue topping the dome, looks small from I-95 but he's 11 feet tall and weighs over 500 pounds. He's made out of an old statue of Simone Bolivar, which once stood in New York's Central Park.

It will always be known as the Big Blue Bug even though it was crowned with the classy name of Nibbles Woodaway in 1990. The name Big Blue Bug just fits; weighing in at 4,000 pounds, this overgrown termite is 9-feet tall and 58-feet long. Guarding the home of New England Pest Control since the 1980's, it's unwittingly become a media darling getting mentions on the likes of The Oprah Winfrey Show, The Today Show and others.

A Desert in Rhode Island

If you look quickly as you pass near Exit 6, close to MP 19, you might catch a glimpse of acres of barren sand on the north side of the interstate..

No one seems to know why it's there. Most locals don't even give it a second thought. To them it's just those sand dunes where kids ride dirt bikes.

What do President Gerald Ford and Astronaut Sally Ride have in common with Plato?

They are all inductees in the International Scholar Athlete Hall of Fame, located near I-95 at Exit 3.

The name explains their mission: to recognize people who have demonstrated excellence as scholars and athletes but also who have shown uncommon "humanitarian achievements" as well.

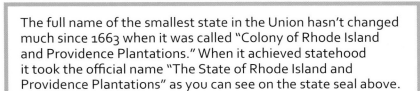
HOPE

In short – the state motto.

There's no lengthy explanation, even on the state's web site.

More than a motto, it's also the name of a town, a valley and an island.

But, while there's Hope, there's also Despair.

Not far away is Patience, Prudence and, of course, Providence.

The full name of the smallest state in the Union hasn't changed much since 1663 when it was called "Colony of Rhode Island and Providence Plantations." When it achieved statehood it took the official name "The State of Rhode Island and Providence Plantations" as you can see on the state seal above.

RHODE ISLAND RED

Naturally this is the state bird.

Rhode Island breeders are credited with developing this distinctive chicken, known for good egg laying and a strong constitution.

Besides that, it's a handsome bird. Breeders know how to accentuate their signature color.

CONNECTICUT

New Haven
New London
Mystic
Old Saybrook

Mystic Seaport

As you cross the bridge near MP 100 and strain to catch a glimpse of historic Mystic Seaport, schooners' masts may be all you can see from the interstate. Northbound travelers can stop briefly at the Jerome Hoxie Scenic Overlook for a better view of the recreated 19th-century seafaring village. It's still a distant vantage point but one that the well-known artist Hoxie himself may have used for inspiration.

Charles W. Morgan

If you're lucky, you might see the village's famous resident, Charles W. Morgan.

Named for a whaler and businessman, the Charles W. Morgan is the only surviving Yankee whaling ship out of over 2,000 built in the 1800's. It sailed the seas for 80 years pursuing bowhead, right and sperm whales.

POST 98

GROTON

Groton's long history started in the mid-1600's when John Winthrop settled in the area. His son, born in Groton, England, became governor of Connecticut. When the town of New London divided in 1705, the new town took the name Groton.

Tales of the area's early settlement and the developing shipbuilding trade fill history books about Groton but the town is busy making history in modern times as the world's leader in building submarines.

Electric Boat (now a division of General Dynamics) formed in 1899 with the purpose of building a submersible craft. Accomplishing their mission a year later, the company went on to develop the world's first nuclear submarine, the Nautilus, which was underway in 1954. The historic and record-shattering Nautilus was decommissioned in 1980 and, in a dignified retirement at Groton, can be toured for free at the The U.S. Navy Submarine Force Museum and Library.

Groton is called the Submarine Capital of the World.

New London, right next door, is home to the United States Coast Guard Academy.

The signs for the Florence Griswold Museum at Exit 70 (MP 80) don't even
hint at the artistic energy generated at this 1817 mansion in Lyme.
Quick history: prosperous family hits hard times; all die but the daughter,
Florence, who takes in boarders to pay the bills.
Then fate moved in. A prominent landscape artist, Henry Ranger, just back
from a tour in Europe, took a room in the Griswold house. Overcome with
the entrancing beauty of the area, he attracted other artists and, long story
short, Florence's house became the center of what was called alternatively
the American Impressionism School and the American Giverny.

How smart is this?

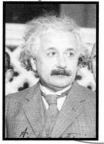

Albert
Einstein
had a
cottage in
Old Lyme.

Old Saybrook, at Exit 69 (MP 78), is proud of its longtime resident Katharine Hepburn. A hurricane that blasted this area in 1938 washed her home off a cliff near here and nearly took Katharine with it.
She lost almost all of her possessions including an Oscar she received six years earlier. That was one of four Best Actress Oscars she earned over her 73-year career, more than any other actor before or since.

"*The Oxbow,*" shown on the left, is a stunning 1836 painting by Thomas Cole that depicts a section of the Connecticut River.
It was inspired by nearby views but is not exhibited at the museum.

That brings up a question:
Which came first, the name of the state or the name of the river? The answer lies in the derivation of the word "Connecticut," a corruption of the Indian word meaning long tidal river.

Good description.

At 400 miles long, it's the longest river in New England, but you might notice there are no huge cities crowding the mouth of this major waterway. A constantly shifting sandbar guards the one-mile mouth of the river like a nervous goalie and makes navigation a nightmare for huge tankers.

50 MILE

Feel like fishing?

Lake Saltonstall near MP 50 is a good place to do it.
The lake, 113 feet deep in some places, is home to trophy bass.
But who was the lake named for?

- Nathaniel Saltonstall was one of seven judges chosen to preside over the Massachusetts witch trials in the 1600's.

- His son Gurdon Saltonstall was governor of Connecticut for 16 years.

- Gurdon's son, Gurdon Jr., married into the Winthrop family whose ancestors founded Massachusetts Bay Colony.

- His son Dudley Saltonstall led the colony's naval forces during the Revolutionary War but was dismissed for negligence.

- Leaverett Saltonstall served as governor of Massachusetts in the early 1940's and is the last Saltonstall to serve as governor in New England.

Their family lineage is the very definition of Boston Brahmins:
the elite of Boston society with historical family trees.
Which Saltonstall do you think the lake was named for?

Near MP 48 there is a sign naming the Pearl Harbor Memorial Bridge. But everybody here knows it as the Q Bridge for the Quinnipiac River it crosses over.

Originally designed for 90,000 cars per day, it now accommodates over 150,000. The recent reconstruction should make it an easier fit.

POST 45

Founded in 1701 as the Collegiate School, Yale University was renamed in 1718 for Elihu Yale, a wealthy Welsh merchant whose generous donation helped keep the school afloat. The ivy league university, less than a mile from the interstate, is the alma mater of a range of success stories from presidents to actors to CEOs.

This claim is hotly contested but if you're from Connecticut, there is no argument: Louis Lassen created the first hamburger in 1900. Louis' grandson, Ken, still broils hamburgers on the original vertical grill at tiny Louis' Lunch on Crown Street close to Yale University, shown to the right. True to his granddaddy's style, catsup and mustard are completely forbidden – it disguises the real hamburger taste.

HORSESHOE CRABS

JUST FLIP 'EM

As you nudge New Haven Harbor, there's something to think about other than traffic. In that bay, and similar waterways from Maine to the Yucatan, are prehistoric horseshoe crabs. They are resilient animals that predate dinosaurs and look like scorpions with armor. But they have an enemy – people harvest tens of thousands of them for eel bait. The eels are then used to catch striped bass. It's the age-old dilemma of usefulness versus ecology and battles rage on both sides. Some local beaches are now off-limits to horseshoe crab hunting.

There's another problem though – surf. Up to 10% of horseshoe crabs die every year simply by being upended by rough surf. Then they get stuck. There is a program underway to "Just Flip 'Em" if you happen upon a stranded horseshoe crab. You could save a life.

P.T. BARNUM

Many people associate that name with the circus. And rightly so. But there was much more to the man than that.

Barnum was a master of promotion, a champion showman and a tireless huckster. He made and lost fortunes. He had a serious side too: he was elected to the Connecticut Legislature in 1865 and Bridgeport's mayor in 1875.

Always appreciative of good publicity, when 81-year-old Barnum felt death was near, he permitted the local newspaper to print his obituary early so he could read all about it.

Just west of the P.T. Barnum bridge you'll see the red-hued P.T. Barnum Museum, which stands out on the north side of I-95 amid more modern structures.

THAT'S NOT BARNUM'S ONLY BRIDGEPORT CONNECTION

Barnum's biggest act, 25-inch tall 5-year old Charles Stratton (aka General Tom Thumb), was born in Bridgeport. At 11 years of age, Charles started growing again and reached a height of 3'4" tall.

The Wright Brothers achieved the first motorized flight at Kitty Hawk, NC, right?

Well, not necessarily. There are serious people who disagree.

It just might be that Gustave Whitehead beat the brothers by more than two years in the airplane pictured above.

The statistics tell the tale: the Wright Brothers flew 852 feet on December 17, 1903. Pretty impressive.

But Whitehead's stats look better. He managed to fly a full 2,625 feet on August 14, 1901.

Whitehead had neither cheering crowds nor photographers to record the event. Newspapers of the day reported the achievement after the fact and Popular Aviation Magazine thought it was a credible enough story to report on in 1935, comparing that account with the Wright Brothers. Gustave came out on top.

This and dozens of other flights happened a short distance south of MP 25 just beyond the rest area.

Mabel Wright was concerned with flight of a different variety. After founding the Connecticut Audubon Society, in 1914 she established the Birdcraft Sanctuary near the rest area at MP 25. It's still in operation and welcomes visitors – with wings and without.

Ms. Wright, a well-known author of children's books and books on nature, was an active citizen of Fairfield at the time of Gustave Whitehead's aerial trials.

Purchase of Norwalk, CT

The name Norwalk sounds English but it's from an Algonquian word meaning "point of land."

YANKEE DOODLE started here in Norwalk, so the legend says.

Here's the story:

In 1756, Connecticut men responded to the call-to-arms for the French and Indian War sometimes straight from their fields . When they reported for duty at the Norwalk residence of Colonel Thomas Fitch, their lack of uniforms bothered Fitch's 16-year old sister.

She helped by sticking chicken feathers in their caps but when the men met up with the smartly outfitted British soldiers, the embellishments were ridiculed. A British surgeon, who was particularly amused, made up a taunting song right then and there. "Yankee Doodle went to town, riding on a pony. Stuck a feather in his hat and called it macaroni." It didn't refer to pasta but rather fanciful dress.

The British smugly chanted the song on the first day of the Revolutionary War. At the end of the war, in 1781, the Yankees escorted the defeated Brits out of Yorktown while proudly singing Yankee Doodle.

About 200 years later it officially became Connecticut's state song.

From the original Yankee Doodle song sheet in the Library of Congress.

From the interstate, the only hint of this piece of history is near MP 16 where the Yankee Doodle Bridge transports you over the Norwalk River.

DARIEN

According to CNN's 2008 list of highest-earning towns, three of the top five richest places in the U.S. are in this corner of Connecticut. Topping the list was New Canaan, second is Darien, and fifth is Westport.

In 1872, John Frederick Kensett painted *Twilight on the Sound, Darien, Connecticut*, shown above.

But listen to this: Darien's Post 53, headquartered near the southbound ramp of Exit 10, is the nation's only EMS run and operated by high school students. Serious training starts at age 14 for the few who make the cut.

When a 911 call comes in, police trained in emergency procedures are the first on the scene. Within minutes, Post 53 arrives to handle Basic Life Support plus some Advanced Life Support. The Stamford EMS steps up if there is a more dire emergency.

LOCKWOOD MATHEWS MANSION

Cradled in the northeast ramp of Exit 15 is one of best examples of Second Empire Style houses left in the U.S. Travelers may be able to glimpse the upper floor of the 62-room mansion, which was nearly demolished in the 1950's. Yeah, yeah – but the fun part is that it was used in filming the 2004 movie The Stepford Wives.

SPLIT ROCK

Blood was spilled in 1643 just a few feet from the path of today's I-95 near a 25-foot glacial boulder called Split Rock. Settler Sarah Hutchinson and her family were attacked and killed here by angry Indians.

This enormous round rock, as tall as a two-story building, is split in two - the double domes permanently agape like a big Pac Man.

In the 1950's, a new throughway (now called I-95) was designed to go right over Split Rock. A successful petition to reroute the roadbed 50 feet saved the rock from a stick of dynamite.

The rock is hard to see, nestled in the underbrush several feet from the road but with sharp eyes you might catch a glimpse as you pass on the interstate. Southbound, it is adjacent to the Exit 14 ramp, on your left (across on-coming traffic), immediately before the bridge over the parkway.

Northbound it's trickier to pinpoint since there is no exit ramp but less than a mile after Exit 13, immediately after the bridge crossing over Hutchinson River Parkway, look for Split Rock on the right.

DOZENS OF FAMILIAR NAMES ARE IN WOODLAWN CEMETERY
Some of them just seem to belong together.

Franklin Woolworth - founder of the five-and-dime store.

James Cash Penney - better know as J.C. Penney

Rowland Macy - started Macy's department store, of course, but you might not know this: before getting into retail he sailed on a whaling ship and, like many good sailors, got a tattoo. His was a red star, which became inspiration for the logo of his store.

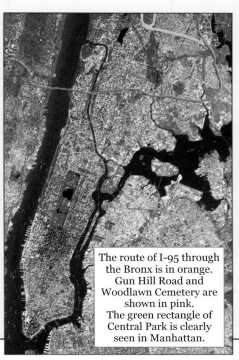

Exactly what road is this?

I-95 has an identity crisis; in its 23-mile journey through New York, its name changes at least three times.

Mileposts are equally schizophrenic and usually nonexistent but for the purpose of identification for this book, "NE Trwy" numbers will do. Exit 10, in that case, corresponds with the milepost number NE 1.

The route of I-95 through the Bronx is in orange. Gun Hill Road and Woodlawn Cemetery are shown in pink. The green rectangle of Central Park is clearly seen in Manhattan.

GUN HILL ROAD

The road at Exit 10, once called Kingsbridge Road because it led to the King's bridge, was always an important artery through the Bronx.

Both British and colonial soldiers wanted control of the road during the Revolutionary War and this led to a skirmish. While the British advanced east, colonial soldiers hauled a cannon up Kingsbridge to the crest of a hill and fired on the enemy, causing them to retreat. Years later the road was renamed Gun Hill Road to memorialize that act of bravery.

Woodlawn Cemetery now encompasses the exact spot of the cannon's perch, about two miles west of I-95. Over 300,000 souls rest in the Bronx's famous cemetery whose site was chosen in 1863. Then it was far from civilization – a peaceful bit of property in the middle of nowhere.

THE PULASKI SKYWAY

The graceful elevated highway that crosses paths with the Turnpike near MP 108 has shaped the New Jersey landscape since 1932.

GENERAL PULASKI MEMORIAL DAY

SINCE 1929

Young Casimir Pulaski came to this country from Poland to fight in the Revolutionary War because he strongly believed in our quest for freedom. But his life was cut short. At age 31 he took British fire and died soon after on October 11, 1779.
The date is now officially General Pulaski Memorial Day.

200,000,000 years ago. Let that sink in.

Travelers who choose the eastern spur of the turnpike can see, between exits 15W and 16W, a graffiti-marked hill with a colorful history. It started 200,000,000 years ago as molten lava that was forced through existing sandstone.

Snake Hill is its name.

In recent history the rock was 150 feet tall and supported a host of buildings including a penitentiary and hospital for the insane. The buildings, as you can see, are gone and much of the mountain is too. Before it was hacked away, though, an ad man, Mortimer Remington, was inspired by the rock. It represented the strength and stability of his client, Prudential Insurance. The rock of Gibraltar is a glorified stand-in but the rock of Secaucus was the original deal.

NEWARK LIBERTY INTERNATIONAL AIRPORT

Near MP 103 a sign announces the airport's new name, changed to memorialize the awful events of September 11, 2001.

That day Flight 93 pulled away from the Newark terminal heading to San Francisco but was destined to crash in a Pennsylvania field at the hands of terrorists. The name references our country's enduring liberty and also its symbol, the Statue of Liberty, just seven miles to the east.

Once the world's busiest airport, now over 36 million travelers take off from here every year. Most of them probably don't know that aviation's best-known female pilot, Amelia Earhart, dedicated Newark Airport's Administration Building in 1935.

For about eight miles, I-95 splits in two from approximately MP 108 to MP 116. The eastern spur is about a half mile longer. Whichever route you travel, parcels of the meadowlands are clearly visible from your car as is the other spur of the turnpike.

Both spurs of the turnpike ride an elevated path through the swampy Meadowlands. This ecologically important wetland once struggled with pollutants but today lives peacefully with horse racing, New York Giants football and concerts at the Meadowlands Racetrack.

Now the wetlands are clean enough to attract the yellow-crowned night heron.

Good luck spotting the "DRIVE SAFELY" tank along the turnpike.

On the west side of the road near MP 98 is a tank farm amid many tank farms. Colonial Pipeline Company is unique in that, as they state on their company web site, it moves more refined petroleum more miles than any other pipeline in the world.

Much of their crude is pumped out of the Gulf of Mexico and processed in Houston. From there, various grades of petroleum products (gasoline, diesel, aviation fuel and home heating oil) are loaded into the pipeline.

At a pace of three to five miles per hour, it takes about 18 days to reach the final destination, here in New Jersey.

A large sign facing the turnpike says
"Linden CoGeneration Plant."
What exactly does that mean?

The company makes energy using five gas turbine generators, which produce a lot of heat.

The heat is turned into steam, which runs the steam generators.

Simple recycling.

POST 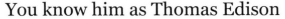 95 88

THE ICE AGE AND NEW JERSEY

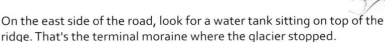

While much of New England groaned under the weight of thousands of feet of ice, here – almost exactly at the Perth Amboy exit – the ice stopped.

On the New Jersey map to the right, the light green shading indicates the coverage of the glacier.

The dark green line shows its southern limit. Near MP 89 just north of Exit 10, the turnpike passes through a deep road cut in the ridge marking the front of the terminal moraine, or a belt of debris (rocks, gravel and sand) left by the retreating glacier.

On the east side of the road, look for a water tank sitting on top of the ridge. That's the terminal moraine where the glacier stopped.

You know him as Thomas Edison

For a kid who attended school for only a brief period of time, Tommy Edison did all right for himself.

He always credited his mother, who home schooled him, for his success.

He had plenty of successes. Edison started well over a hundred companies with a variety of endeavors: telegraph, phonograph, electric light, railway, battery and even torpedoes. Not all of his companies were long lived but many, like General Electric, were.

Some of his greatest ideas were hatched near here in Menlo Park; the phonograph, electric light and the first system for distributing light and power, and telephone transmitter. That's why he's honored with a southbound turnpike service area named after him.

WOODROW WILSON

This Princeton grad became the United States' 28th President but as a kid, he couldn't read until the age of 12. Despite that, he earned a PhD from Johns Hopkins University and, as president, started the Federal Reserve System. He also proclaimed Mothers Day to be a national holiday. The service area near MP 59 northbound is named for Wilson who also served as Governor of New Jersey.

THE FRENCH CONNECTION: Part One
Richard Stockton's family members were, at different times, disgraced and befriended by the French.

Richard Stockton, a signer of the Declaration of Independence, is honored along the Turnpike with a southbound service area named after him. But his individual story is not nearly as interesting as his family history.

Richard's grandson, Robert Stockton, became a New Jersey senator and fast friends with Joseph Bonaparte, brother of Napoleon, King of France.

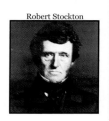
Robert Stockton

Here's the ironic twist: While his friend Bonaparte came to the States to escape persecution in France, so did Stockton's ancestors, for quite different reasons.

Robert Stockton's great-great-great grandparents were Protestants living in France in 1687 when the King of France, Louis XIV, set out to eliminate all non-Catholics. Their lives were spared by escaping to the colonies.

Where did I-95 go?

You can't drive from New York to Delaware continuously on I-95. The two ends of the designated I-95 road are 10 miles from each other, like two live wires waving in the air. Although the federal highway system recognizes parts of the New Jersey Turnpike as I-95, there are few signs to confirm that.

Since the missing section is in PA, it's up to PennDot to bridge the gap. They're working on it.

THE FRENCH CONNECTION: Part Two
France's Bonaparte family lands in Bordentown.

Joseph may have stood out on Bordentown's streets in this get-up.

Napoleon Bonaparte, emperor of France, was defeated at Waterloo in 1815 and exiled to a small island. His brother Joseph, King of Spain, tried to convince him to flee to the United States. Napoleon declined but Joseph, under an assumed name, took the steamer to New York. Looking for a peaceful haven, he settled in Bordentown where he was a friendly and gregarious neighbor for about two decades. He entertained lavishly. Some of his guests are familiar names even today; Henry Clay, Daniel Webster, John Quincy Adams, Commodore Robert Stockton.

31 🛡NJ 95 MILE

Walt Whitman

Exit 3 takes you to the Walt Whitman Bridge but you don't have to get off the turnpike to find a place dedicated to one of America's best-known poets. The southbound service center near MP 31 honors Whitman who was born on Long Island, but lived and died in Camden just a few miles from here.

New Jersey is one of 17 states that chose the honeybee as their state insect. Essential in the pollination of food crops, New Jersey's apples, melons, pumpkins and peaches depend on the little bees.

But bee colonies are in jeopardy. Colony Collapse Disorder, or CCD, is decimating hives all over the U.S. Despite scientific research, no one has conclusively figured out why the colonies are failing.

POST 26

Exit 3 at MP 26 is a lot more exciting than it looks.

For one thing, in Haddonfield just a few miles west of the turnpike there was a discovery of earth shaking proportions...

Imagine the surprise of William Foulke, a member of the Philadelphia Academy of Natural Sciences, when he showed up to a dinner party in Haddonfield in 1858. In the front hall was an umbrella stand that looked like an enormous fossilized leg bone. "That old thing?" his host might have said. "There's a lot more where that came from and it's just down the street."

In the following days, Foulke excavated the area and retrieved a nearly complete dinosaur skeleton, the first found in the entire world.

Named Hadrosaurus foulkii, its bones were mounted into a lifelike pose soon after its discovery and put on display. It can still be seen at the Philadelphia Academy of Natural Sciences.

A ten-year campaign by a local schoolteacher and her students resulted in the Hadrosaurus becoming the state's official dinosaur.

JERSEY SHORE

Exit 3 is your portal to Atlantic City, about 50 miles to the east. Once there, you are in the center of the Jersey Shore, a region extending from Asbury Park to Cape May on the southern tip of the peninsula.

Bruce Springsteen started his singing career along the Jersey Shore. If you're quiet long enough, you can almost hear refrains of "Born in the USA."

No matter where they live or where they're coming from, a New Jersey native says they're "going down the shore" if they are headed toward the beach.

Harrisburg

83

PENNSYLVANIA

76

MARYLAND

4
Wilmington
Edgemoor

Rising Sun   5

Havre De Grace   6

7   Aberdeen

Baltimore

8

95

Dover

Washington DC
9   Annapolis

Andrews AFB

DELAWARE

Holmesburg

Philadelphia

Behind the walls...

Holmesburg Prison lurks along the interstate near MP 31 just begging to be cast in another movie. The prison, which opened in 1896, was already featured in two motion pictures – *Up Close and Personal* and *Animal Factory*.

Seen from I-95, the 35-foot high walls enclose a facility that housed inmates until 1995. At that time the outdated prison was replaced by the modern Curran-Fromhold Correctional Facility just south of the old prison, on the east side of the highway. But that wasn't the end to the old building's story; in 2006 the new place overflowed with prisoners and 80 of them were relocated to Holmesburg Prison.

POST 95 27

Who was Elizabeth Griscom Ross Ashburn Claypoole?

She was a Philadelphia girl who worked as an upholsterer **during the tumultuous years of our country's birth.** She knew George Washington. **In fact, her pew in Christ Church was next to his.** Elizabeth went by the name Betsy.

In most circles, Betsy Ross is credited with sewing the first flag of the young **United States at the request of George Washington.** That doesn't make her a vexillologist, however. **That's a flag expert or someone who studies flags.** The name comes from the Romans who carried *vexilla*, ancient military standards.

> Near MP 27 you cross under the Betsy Ross Bridge,
> the first major bridge dedicated to a woman.

18th Century Collides with Modern Needs

You'd never guess what is just behind the concrete barrier on the west side of the road by MP 22 (very near the southern side of the Benjamin Franklin Bridge abutment).

It's Elfreth's Alley - one of our nation's oldest streets.

Three hundred years ago this section of Philadelphia pulsed with activity, as it does today. The docks welcomed ships from around the

world, taverns hopped and shops were crowded. A strip of land called Elfreth's Alley opened up in 1702 to connect the wharf with busy 2nd Street. Homes soon lined the alley.

Two hundred and fifty years later, in the 1950's, a growing Philadelphia needed an interstate highway and the preferred path went right over the one-block long Elfreth's Alley. The Elfreth's Alley Association helped preserve this living, breathing residential block, in continuous use since the early 1700's.

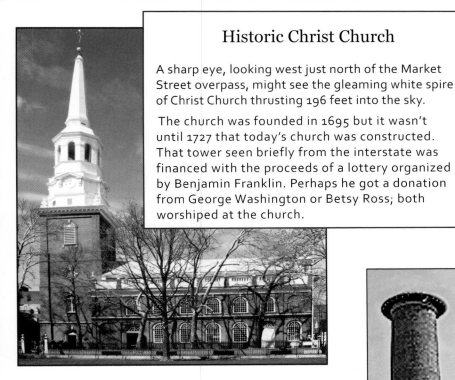

Historic Christ Church

A sharp eye, looking west just north of the Market Street overpass, might see the gleaming white spire of Christ Church thrusting 196 feet into the sky.

The church was founded in 1695 but it wasn't until 1727 that today's church was constructed. That tower seen briefly from the interstate was financed with the proceeds of a lottery organized by Benjamin Franklin. Perhaps he got a donation from George Washington or Betsy Ross; both worshiped at the church.

SPARKS SHOT TOWER

Thank the Brits for that brick tower seen along I-95 near MP 20.

At the dawn of the 19th century, hunters and militia depended mostly on musket balls and shot imported from Great Britain.

As political tension mounted, so did the price of shot.

Just about that time, it was discovered that dropping molten lead from a high perch into water below would make perfectly round ammunition.

In 1808 Thomas Sparks, a plumber who hunted to put food on the table, built one of America's first shot towers. At 142-feet in height, it and Christ Church were the tallest structures in Philadelphia.

Business boomed during the War of 1812. The tower was used to make ammunition until 1903.

17 🛡️**95** MILE

Philly Naval Yard

If the last new ship was built at the Navy Yard in 1970 (and it was) then why are those mammoth ships parked over there near MP 17?

In 1995 the Navy Yard, the U.S. Navy's first naval shipyard, became a commercial shipyard but, in part, the facility now houses the Naval Inactive Ship Maintenance Facility, which cares for decommissioned ships in their retirement years.

Philadelphia Airport

Getting 500,000 airplanes out of Philadelphia International Airport every year is routine now but when Charles Lindbergh dedicated the airport in 1927 it was little more than a grassy strip of land. But it grew quickly. By 1940 the Philadelphia Municipal Airport, as it was called then, served 40,000 passengers. That number has swelled to about 30 million annually.

Heinz Wildlife Refuge

On the west side of the interstate, directly opposite the airport, is an important refuge for birds who stop here to grab a bite and rest their wings during spring and fall migrations.

As far back as 1634, people tried to tame the marshland seen along the interstate at MP 10 – 13. Original settlers (Swedes, Dutch and English) used dikes to make the ground solid for grazing livestock and building houses.

Over the years, civilization nibbled at the marshes but the biggest threat loomed with plans for Interstate 95. One proposed route went directly through the last 200 acres of freshwater tidal marsh in Pennsylvania. Senator John Heinz successfully fought to preserve the Tinicum Marsh and that's why the interstate snuggles up so close to the airport as you can see in the picture on the left.

John Heinz was honored in 1991 with the renaming of the marsh, now called the John Heinz National Wildlife Refuge.

Their baseball team is singing the blues, but it's a good thing.

The 6,532-seat Frawley Stadium near MP 14 south of Exit 6 is home to the Wilmington Blue Rocks, an affiliate of the Kansas City Royals. It's so close to I-95 you might catch a fly ball on your way past.

In any other city a team called the Blue Rocks may seem unusual but in Wilmington it makes perfect sense. Just ask their mascot Rocky Bluewinkle.

He'd tell you about construction workers who cracked open a normal-looking rock that was a rich royal blue inside. Geologists call it Brandywine Blue Gneiss of the Wilmington Complex but the locals here mostly call it Blue Rocks. They underlie much of this area including the path of I-95 near the stadium.

Delaware

An odd coincidence - Delaware has also been called the "Blue Hen State", referring to the official state bird, the Blue Hen Chicken, which was carried with the Delaware Revolutionary War soldiers for cockfighting.

Zelda and Scott Fitzgerald

F. Scott Fitzgerald worked on his novel *Tender is the Night* in the late 1920's while living in a mansion (now gone) in the town of Edgemoor, due east of Exit 8 at MP 16.

His distant cousin was a lawyer forced to witness the bombing of Baltimore, Maryland by British ships in 1814. Afterwords, the cousin wrote a stirring poem about the experience. The novelist's full name was Francis Scott Key Fitzgerald, named after his famous relative.

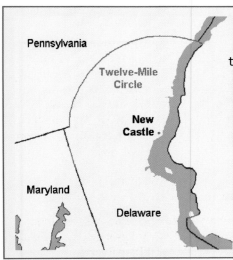

Pennsylvania

Twelve-Mile Circle

New Castle

Maryland

Delaware

Did you ever wonder why most of the boundary between Delaware and Pennsylvania is a perfect arc? The deed William Penn obtained in 1682 stipulated the area be measured in a twelve-mile circle centered on the "Towne of Newcastle."

New Castle is about 3.5 miles southeast of I-95 at Exit 5.

Delaware is called "The First State" because it was. On December 7, 1787, Delaware delegates were the first to ratify the U.S. Constitution.

Lord de la Warr

In 1610, the suffering pioneers in Jamestown, Virginia trudged to their ships intending to go home to the British Isles. Just in the nick of time, Lord de la Warr arrived by boat from England and escorted them back to Jamestown to give it another go. De la Warr engaged in the First Anglo-Powhatan War, which ended in a peace treaty. This opened the continent up for further settlement.
The state, river, bay and even the Indian tribe are named after him.

John F. Kennedy Memorial Highway

The border between Delaware and Maryland offered the perfect photo op on November 14, 1963. It was the bicentennial of the start of Mason and Dixon's famous survey. Coincidentally, near the spot of the laying of the first marker, a section of interstate highway was set to open. Although no president had ever personally dedicated a road opening, John Kennedy joined in the ribbon cutting at the border. His next public appearance was eight days later in Dallas, TX where he was assassinated.

Hey, wait a minute. I-95 doesn't cross the Mason-Dixon line!
That's north of here; it's the border between Pennsylvania and Maryland.

Well, yes and no.

Everyone knows "The Line" determines the PA/MD border but fewer people know that the surveyors were also called on to measure the border between Maryland and Delaware. Although it's not mentioned on official signage, I-95 crosses the Mason-Dixon line at the border of the two states.

But take a close look at the map. As a result of their survey and the Twelve-Mile Circle, there were some odd results. For instance, The Wedge. For a time it was possible to stand with one foot in Maryland, one foot in Delaware with Pennsylvania right between your legs. That minor detail was ironed out in 1892 when Delaware got that slice of the pie.

With a name like Rising Sun, the town must have a good story.

Here's the short version: a popular tavern/inn along a main road southwest out of Philadelphia had an identifying sign hanging out front with the words "The Rising Sun" and an image of sun rays at daybreak. 19th century travelers often planned to "meet at the Rising Sun." The village of Summer Hill grew up around the tavern.

The town was in Pennsylvania, or so most people thought.
After Mason and Dixon established a firm border, the town was in Maryland.

The tavern became such a popular place to meet that when the town was officially named in 1815, it was called Rising Sun, now at Exit 100.

Other odd conditions materialized with the laying of the line. This stone, one of the originals, marks a segment that goes right through the middle of the church.

The question here is, which came first - the line or the church?

A SMALL PIECE OF CIVIL WAR HISTORY

The unassuming white house on the west side of the road at MP 105 is the boyhood home of a Confederate General. William Whann Mackall grew up here, then went on to study at West Point in 1837. After showing leadership in the Seminole and Mexican Wars, he was offered a military position with the Union forces but instead joined the Confederacy where he rose to the rank of General.

91 MILE

CHESAPEAKE, THE BAY AND THE RIVER

You get a fleeting glimpse of the Chesapeake Bay about midway over the Millard Tydings Bridge. The Bay is the result of global warming 10,000 years ago. Before that, during the last ice age, the Susquehanna River emptied out here into a valley. As the ice melted, the ocean levels rose and flooded the valley, creating today's Chesapeake Bay. Crossword buffs might like to know that the word for that geological phenomenon is "ria."

If you look the other way, to the west, there is a beautiful view of the Susquehanna River. After a journey of 444 miles from the upper reaches of Pennsylvania and New York, the river widens and slows to a leisurely pace before merging with the brackish waters of the Chesapeake. The Susquehanna River provides about half of the Chesapeake's fresh water.

Havre de Grace and the Decoy Museum

France's Marquis de Lafayette was so taken with the beauty of this area he suggested the name Havre de Grace, or Harbor of Mercy. The citizens took his advice but now sometimes shorten it to HdG.

In the early 1900's it was especially attractive to waterfowl, particularly Canvasback Ducks. The skies were filled with birds that loved to rest in the shallow Susquehanna Flats.

Hunters flocked here too and, to help lure the birds within shooting distance, they used hand carved decoys. The increasing popularity of duck hunting led to a thriving cottage industry of decoy carving and that history is celebrated today at the Decoy Museum. But it's not an art lost to history books. Today, Havre de Grace harbors many carvers who are also occasionally highlighted at the museum.

The sign along I-95 at Exit 89 is so tiny it hardly hints at the importance decoy making was, and still is, to this area.

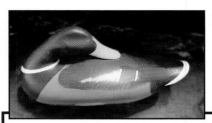

Mallard

Millard

Millard E. Tydings Bridge

The bridge at MP 91 is dedicated to Havre de Grace native Millard E. Tydings. He won 4 U.S. Senate elections and served Maryland from 1927 to 1951, nearly 25 years.

You can bet he enjoyed a few days cruising the Susquehanna Flats hunting ducks.

Aberdeen Proving Ground
What are they proving in Aberdeen?

In essence they are proving that the army is ready for action. Here at the army's oldest such facility, they test military equipment, technology and even tactics.

Drama even Shakespeare couldn't top.

Junius Brutus Booth, a renowned English actor, moved to the U.S. in 1821. His talent as a superb Shakespearean actor won him acclaim from New York to New Orleans to San Francisco. His family lived on an isolated farm about 7 miles west of today's Exit 85.

Junius built a Gothic-Revival cottage complete with a small balcony to practice dramatic elocution and dubbed the house "Tudor Hall."

That alone might be newsworthy but here's the catch: in May of 1838 his son John was born in this house. That boy grew to be more infamous than his father. John Booth assassinated Abraham Lincoln.

The saga of the house is almost as interesting as the family's tale.

Years after John's horrific deed, his mother sold the house in 1878 for $3,500. The house transferred title several times over the years and ended up in the hands of a couple who knew nothing of its history. It went up for auction in 2006. Hartford County's winning bid was a staggering $810,000. Now the county safely guards the house and its history.

They love their baseball heroes in Maryland.

As you pass near MP 85, you see a little piece of the heart of Aberdeen on the west side of the road. That's Ripken Stadium's scoreboard and right field fence, all that's visible from I-95 of the Aberdeen Complex.

The Maryland baseball dynasty started with Cal Ripken Sr. who spent 36 years in baseball (player, manager, coach), many for the Baltimore Orioles where he managed his own two sons, Billy and Cal Jr.

Young Cal Jr., born in nearby Havre de Grace, went on to become a legend. Playing out his whole career in Baltimore, he tops the record books in consecutive games played. At 2,632, the record far surpasses the #2 spot, Lou Gehrig's 2,130.

Before hitting the big league, a 20-year-old Cal Jr. played in the longest professional baseball game. In a triple-A International League game, Cal played for the Rochester Red Wings in a game that spanned multiple days and lasted a total of 8 hours, 25 minutes. Although there were 219 at-bats, the score was 3-2.

The Red Wings won.

First, some history about Ft. McHenry

Set the stage: Britain and France were at war. American ships were often the subject of search and seizure. Sometimes the crew was even forced to fight for the Royal Navy. Finally, America threw down the gauntlet and declared war on Britain, starting the War of 1812.

Baltimore, a thriving city of 50,000, prepared for an attack. The commanding officer wanted a flag flying from Baltimore's fort that was big enough for the Brits to see from a distance.
Mary Pickersgill got to work on a wool flag that measured 30 feet x 42 feet. It cost $405.90. Now they were ready for war.

Meanwhile a young lawyer, Francis Scott Key, boarded an American truce ship in the harbor to negotiate the release of a captive. Wrong place, wrong time.

When the British battleships arrived, Key was not permitted to leave the ship: he knew too much. On September 13th the bombs started flying. For 25 hours the British lobbed an estimated 1800 shells at Fort McHenry but the fort stood.

"By the dawn's early light" on September 14th, Key could see the huge American flag still waving in the wind.

Ft. McHenry Tunnel

Something had to be done about traffic congestion through Baltimore; that was clear in the 1970's. The less expensive solution was to build a bridge over the Baltimore Harbor. That idea was rejected – a bridge would destroy the view and the impact of Fort McHenry National Monument. At a cost of $750 million ($75 million under budget), the world's largest submerged vehicular tunnel goes almost right underneath the battle site.

Baltimore Orioles, the bird

The small orange and black bird that ranges from Canada to South America at different times of the year was named the Baltimore Oriole because the male's plumage matches the colors on Lord Baltimore's coat-of-arms. The state naturally adopted it as the state bird even though it only summers here.

DUNN, BALTIMORE

Baltimore Orioles, the team

Signs show the way to Oriole Park at Camden Yards but you can't see the stadium from I-95. Baltimore is proud of its baseball heritage with the likes of Orioles Cal Ripken and Babe Ruth, but when the fans rise before a game, do they have an extra sense of pride singing the National Anthem?

Fort McHenry is less than three miles away.

Without Jack Dunn (shown left) there might not have been Babe Ruth. Dunn, owner and manager of the Orioles, saw promise in 19-year-old George Ruth. In order to have the youngster play pro ball, Dunn became Ruth's legal guardian and the other players called him "Jack's newest babe."

Capital Beltway

Southbound as you approach the interchange where I-95 meets I-495, hang on tight. This is one of two interchanges on the Beltway (the ring road around D.C.) that was identified as one of the 20 worst bottlenecks in the nation. About 185,125 cars rush through here daily.

If you are heading north and leaving the gravitational pull of the Beltway, breathe a short sigh of relief.

By the way, the other nearby intersection on the list is closer to the northwest segment of the Beltway where I-495 meets I-270. That one is even worse: it gets up to 243,400 cars a day.

Pennsylvania Avenue and the White House

Pennsylvania Avenue at Exit 11 is sometimes called "America's Main Street." From that exit it's only about ten miles to the White House, home to America's First Family.

Andrews Air Force Base is best known to most civilians as the landing pad for the president's jet, Air Force One. But "The President's Wing" or more correctly called the 89th Airlift Wing, is only part of this base. Over 20,000 people work here, including active duty military personnel, civilian employees and their families.

Why does a map of D.C. look like a broken block?

Our country's leaders decided to locate the center of the nation's government here, in a 100-square mile area. Maryland and Virginia gave, or ceded, their land and D.C. was a perfect square. The District of Columbia was open for business November 1800.

In the deal, the citizens living on the ceded land lost their right to vote. No elected official directly represented their needs. Still, the system worked for almost fifty years.

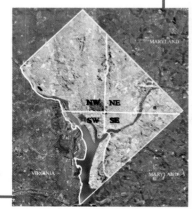

Anti-slavery rumblings in Washington D.C. worried the residents of Alexandria, VA. They relied heavily on the slave trade, as did the rest of Virginia. In 1847 those citizens voted to retrocede their 31 square miles of land. As a result, they won back two representatives who were pro-slavery and D.C.'s square became, well, more irregular.

Maryland's 69 square mile parcel is all that's left.

Washington DC

Alexandria ①

Dumfries ②

Quantico

③ Fredericksburg

Chancellorsville

Ladysmith ④

Richmond ⑤

⑥

Colonial Heights

Petersburg ⑦

Smithfield

Norfolk

⑧

Emporia

INTERESTING INTERSTATES

VIRGINIA

①	MP 178 - 179 Alexandria		Pages 88-89
②	MP 145 - 152 Quantico, Dumfries		Pages 90-91
③	MP 126 - 130 Chancellorsville, Fredericksburg		Pages 92-93
④	MP 98 - 110 Ladysmith		Pages 94-95
⑤	MP 74 Richmond		Pages 96-97
⑥	MP 64 - 69 South of Richmond		Pages 98-99
⑦	MP 52 - 53 Petersburg, Colonial Heights		Pages 100-101
⑧	MP 11 - 28 Emporia, Smithfield		Pages 102-103

As you cross over Wilson Bridge, you are in Washington D.C. for a millisecond between the signs for Virginia and Maryland.

If you're going south, a sweet little cardinal welcomes you to Virginia but a couple of real eagles might be keeping an eye on you too. During years of road construction, two D.C. residents (George and Martha), watched the jackhammers and cement trucks from their perch close to Wilson Bridge. The two bald eagles might appreciate the 84-acre bald eagle sanctuary that was part of the reconstruction project. It's just north of the bridge.

Alexandria and the first death of the Civil War

Zouaves were known for two things. The French soldiers fighting in Northern Africa in the mid-1800's were ferocious in battle and their uniforms were colorful, even comical by today's standards.

Starting before the Civil War, some U.S. volunteer militia adopted the name, the fighting attitude and the flamboyant style of the Zouaves.

Elmer Ellsworth from New York formed his own unit, the New York Fire Zouaves. In the days before the first rally of fire in the Civil War, the Fire Zouaves were stationed in Washington D.C. When news circulated that Virginia voted to secede from the Union, Ellsworth and his men headed to Alexandria to secure the port but a large Confederate flag flying from the top of the Marshall House Inn diverted him. He charged into the building and removed the flag but as he came back down the steps the owner, Jim Jackson, shot him. Elmer Ellsworth was the first casualty of the Civil War.

Shown here is the young fighter, dressed in his Zouave uniform, who ran his bayonet through the man who killed Ellsworth. He is standing on the flag that caused the problem.

POST ![VA 95] 178

Woodrow Wilson Bridge

Before recent improvements to Wilson Bridge, traffic screeched to a halt on I-95 about 260 times a year. The drawbridge cranked open to let boats pass beneath the interstate. Now the bridge deck is nearly 30 feet higher. Only cruise ships, Navy tugs and tall mast ships (like *Peacemaker*, shown here) require an opening, causing a traffic snarl on I-95.

BACKHOES UNEARTH SLAVES' CEMETERY

In laying the first roadbed for Virginia's section of I-95, grading went on without thought to historic relics underground. But near the turn of the 21st century, when I-95 expansion unearthed an old grave site in Alexandria, construction stopped dead.

They discovered the remains of about 1,800 people, slaves who had fled north during the Civil War. The area was reclaimed; an old gas station on the site was torn down, and the buried were given the dignity they lacked in the 1800's.

The site, just yards away from I-95 near the southern end of Wilson Bridge, is called Contrabands and Freedmens Cemetery Memorial. Contraband is an escaped slave and Freedmen are former slaves who had been freed.

Signs says "Safety Corridor."
It's really a "Not As Safe Corridor."

Crash data, traffic volume and highway engineering were evaluated to find the sections of the interstate system where accidents are most likely to occur. This 11-mile section of I-95 qualifies.
Dangerous drivers (speeders, tailgaters, etc.) could face a fine up to $2,500 if stopped in the "I-95 Highway Safety Corridor."

Whatever works.

According to the Virginia Department of Transportation, during a morning commute on I-95 there is a 25% chance that a car in the HOV lane has a slug in it. And everyone is happy about it. Non-Virginians might need an explanation: slugging is a method of carpooling. A slug driver picks up enough strangers to qualify for the HOV lanes. They are the slugs. It works so well that about 3,000 slugs grab free rides each weekday morning.
The name doesn't refer to the slimy bug but rather a dummy coin.

Weems Botts Museum

"If walls could talk," someone said and maybe these walls can; this museum in Dumfries at Exit 152 is thought to be haunted.

Mason Weems, a prolific writer, owned the house at the turn of the 19th century. He wrote biographies of famous people and wasn't above embellishing certain aspects of their lives. For instance, George Washington's biography was jazzed up a bit with a story about young George fatally wounding his father's cherry tree and confessing to the deed. It was a best seller. In fact for many years it was second only to the Holy Bible in sales.

Weems sold the house to Benjamin Botts. His tale is more somber; he was on a team of lawyers who successfully defended Aaron Burr against charges of treason. Burr was accused of conspiring with the Spanish in a plot against the American government.

POST 🛣️ 145

Quantico Marine Base

"Iconic." Although overused, is the perfect word to describe the statue of six United States warriors raising the flag in victory over Iwo Jima. One of the men was a Navy guy. The other five were Marines, the kind who come here to the base at Quantico to learn combat strategies and military professionalism. The original statue is located at Arlington National Cemetery in D.C. but a slightly scaled down version welcomes visitors to the Marine Corps Base Quantico.

It's also the main training facility for the FBI. Remember Agent Starling in *Silence of the Lambs*?

National Museum of the Marine Corps

You get only a fleeting glimpse of the museum from I-95 just south of Exit 150 on the east side of the road even though it's only 500 feet away from the interstate.

Notice in these pictures that the architecture echoes the lines of the Iwo Jima monument.

From boot camp to the flight simulator, the museum helps visitors understand how an ordinary kid is transformed into a sharp and cunning Marine. "Era galleries" demonstrate the Marine's contributions for over 230 years of United States history.

Tom Jackson might not ring a bell but his nickname identifies him.

He earned the name Stonewall Jackson while leading his men during the Battle of Bull Run. Many people, even today, consider him a tactical genius in battle. He was one of the most prominent and successful Confederate leaders; second, perhaps, only to Robert E. Lee.

He proved his prowess for the last time at the Battle of Chancellorsville about 7 miles west of MP 130. In a 5-hour battle, 17,500 soldiers were either shot or captured but Stonewall prevailed. As Jackson rode back to camp on horseback, he was mistaken for a Union soldier by one of his own men. Shots rang out and Jackson was hit in the shoulder. His arm was amputated in the field. A chaplain buried it nearby while Jackson was moved to a more sanitary place for medical assistance. Jackson died eight days later. He was 39 years old. His arm, buried separate from the rest of his body, received its own headstone.

During the Civil War, more battles were fought in Virginia than in any other state.

The Civil War still lives here in Spotsylvania County.

The hills are haunted by the 15,000 men killed and the 80,000 wounded in four major battles that raged within a short distance from today's interstate. The Civil War Life Museum, along I-95 at MP 126, once told the story from only the Confederate soldiers' side. There is always more than one perspective and, after reworking the exhibits, the museum gives a voice to both sides, including soldiers, slaves and civilians.

JEFFERSON DAVIS
President of the Confederacy

Route 1, at Exit 126, has a more colorful past than its name implies.
Around here, it's called Jefferson Davis Highway after the president of the Confederacy.

Here's a short version of the story:

After an auto trail, an early 20th century collection of barely related roads, was grouped into the Lincoln Highway (running from New York to San Francisco) the United Daughters of the Confederacy thought Jefferson Davis should be equally honored. They worked hard to get a chain of roads dedicated to Jefferson, a line that would run south from D.C. into Georgia then cross the country to San Diego. Their efforts failed but Virginia's section still goes by the name Jefferson Davis Highway.

Ladysmith

Ladysmith, the tiny Caroline County community at Exit 110, had some famous neighbors.

- First, in 1770, a boy named William Clark was born in the county, about 15 miles east of here. He later became half of the famous team of explorers known as Lewis and Clark.
- Here's an odd coincidence: Meriwether Lewis, the other half of that team, was born four years after Clark and only 50 miles west of here.
- Everyone remembers John Wilkes Booth who shot President Lincoln while he attended a play in D.C. Booth, of course, escaped and fled south. His pursuers finally caught up to him 20 miles east of this spot on the Garrett's tobacco farm.

This is the porch where lawmen finally caught him. Booth never made it off the front steps.

Virginia IS Old Dominion

If you have dominion over something, you have total and complete control. King Charles II, in 1663, bestowed that status to the settlers of Virginia since he considered them to be the most loyal of all the colonial settlements. The Virginians preferred the name Old Dominion, as Jamestown, VA was the first permanent settlement in the New World.

Kings Dominion

Two million people enjoy Kings Dominion amusement park annually.

Even though two coasters, the Grizzly and the Hurler (seen here) are only about 200 feet from the interstate at MP 98 - and both stand over 80-feet tall - they are completely hidden behind the mature trees. Still, you might hear a rebel yell coming from a downhill slide between March and September.

Secretariat, the Michael Jordan of horse racing.

The fact that super horse Secretariat was sired two miles from MP 98 shouldn't be too much of a surprise. After all, North America's thoroughbred racing started here in Caroline County during colonial times when Arabian horses were imported for breeding racers.

Christopher Chenery, Secretariat's owner, acquired the horse in a lucky flip of the coin – literally. He and another stable owner made a deal: When their horses were bred, no stud fee would be charged if each owner got a colt. The first owner to pick a colt would be decided by a coin toss. Chenery lost and, as the second choice, got the horse he named Secretariat.

Secretariat won the Triple Crown in 1973, setting two records that still stand today.

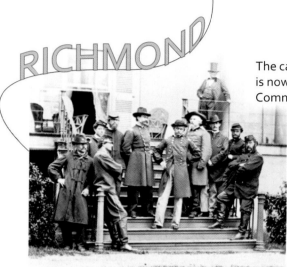

RICHMOND

The capital of the Confederacy is now the capital of the Commonwealth of Virginia.

Here, on the steps of the Confederate White House, Union leaders gathered in the final days of the Civil War. In the south, it's often referred to as The War of Northern Aggression or the War Between the States.

I-95 runs right between two important Richmond buildings.

The Monroe Building was the tallest building in Virginia until 2007 when Virginia Beach acquired a taller complex. This one honors the 5th U.S. President James Monroe, who was born on a Virginia plantation.

From I-95 the clock tower is about all you can see of Richmond's red brick Main Street Station. Built in 1901, it was decommissioned in 1975. Good times are here again! It reopened to train service in 2003.

Edgar Allen Poe was a strange bird.

Although he was born in Boston, died in Baltimore, lived in various places such as NYC and Philadelphia, Edgar Allen Poe lived in Richmond from the time he was a baby through his short stint at the University of Virginia. The University's Raven Society, which honors academic excellence, also honors Poe's most famous poem, The Raven. At the time The Raven was published in 1845, Poe received the handsome sum of $9.00 for his efforts. Converted to today's value, that was more than $200. Not bad but he never got a penny more even though the poem was wildly successful and published throughout the country.

Buried and forgotten, the Devil's Half Acre - and its painful history - now again coming to life.

Everyone knew of Richmond's history as a major port in the business of slavery. In fact, it was second only to New Orleans, processing up to 300,000 enslaved men, women and children. It was a surprise, though, when it was discovered that the remains of the most brutal slave jail, Lumpkin's Devil's Half Acre, was partially beneath I-95. Excavation is underway to unearth the foundation that, today, is practically in the parking lot of Main Street Station.

Triple Crossing

At the northern shore of the James River, there is an oddity that doesn't occur anywhere else in North America: it's the Triple Crossing where three main train lines cross paths in one spot.

Port of Richmond

The Port of Richmond near MP 69 is a small port but it has its advantages. I-95 is one of them. By sailing 78 miles up the James River from Newport News, ships reach the westernmost port on the Atlantic seaboard. After unloading their cargo onto trucks, it's a simple matter to jump on the interstate to deliver the goods inland. Shipments leaving the Port of Richmond might be on their way to Iceland, the Mediterranean or Mexico.

Def Sup Ctr

Def Sup Ctr and Def Dep – what in the world do those signs at Exit 67 mean? If you're not from around here it might sound like gibberish but it stands for Defense Supply Center Richmond and Defense Department Richmond VA. They provide a crucial service to the aviation division of United States military. All divisions (aviation, land and maritime but in this case, aviation) need operational support. Def Sup Ctr manages providers and orchestrates the flow of provisions to be sure there are enough of the right nuts and bolts (and a lot of other things) to keep planes flying.

Phillip Morris' statue

The unmistakable statue near MP 70 is not quite a cigarette but not quite a cigarette pack either. It is an effective advertisement for Phillip Morris & Co., which turned into PM USA, which turned into Altria Group, Inc.

The real Phillip Morris operated a small tobacco shop in London in the mid-1800's. Morris incorporated his popular business and expanded to New York City in 1902. Lately, production has been shrinking slightly. In 2008, the company manufactured "only" 169.4 billion cigarettes. Company headquarters and all manufacturing have recently moved here to Richmond.

KING TOBACCO

When John Rolfe arrived in Virginia in 1612, Indians were already using indigenous tobacco products for ceremonial and medicinal purposes. But Rolfe made a business out of it by introducing a new strain of bright-leaf tobacco (preferred by Englishmen). At the risk of imprisonment, Rolfe imported prized seeds from Trinidad that produced a sweeter, denser leaf.

Luck was with him. Colonial Jamestown was situated perfectly for growing this sweet tobacco. Sandy soil closer to the ocean and clay soil farther inland produced a rougher taste. Still, tobacco was grown in every Virginia county (except for the land that eventually became West Virginia). It took just seven years for tobacco to become the number one export from the Colonies.

In the early years, tobacco was chewed or smoked in a pipe. Cigarettes weren't popular until after the Civil War.

Today, Virginia tobacco production is almost exactly what it was in 1866. Now the same amount of tobacco is produced on much less land. More efficient production methods have reduced acreage devoted to tobacco to one third what it was then. The harvest is also declining due in part to international competition.

Brazil provides a substantial amount of tobacco in today's cigarette blends. Africa, China, the Middle East and even Canada also grow tobacco commercially.

Pocahontas Island

The island you cross over near MP 53 is named for the Powhatan princess Pocahontas. Her father was the supreme ruler of a wide swath of land that included this area.

The island was home to the country's first and largest free black community. There are still two existing homes on the island once used in the Underground Railroad, the secret path that led slaves to freedom.

In 1993, 64 houses remained on the island but an F4 tornado with winds of 250 mph swept through the area damaging every home. Thirty-four had to be torn down. The island barely escaped another tornado fifteen years later. In 2008, an F1 tornado snaked through Colonial Heights less than two miles to the north.

Matoaka is better know as Pocahontas, a playful nickname that meant "little wanton" according to William Strachery, a man who lived in Jamestown.

This 1840 painting by John Chapman shows her baptism and acceptance of Christianity. Here she became known as Rebecca and soon married John Rolfe.

POST ⬡ 95 52

Petersburg National Battlefield

Petersburg National Battlefield is the site of the
Petersburg Siege, a nine-month Union effort to
isolate the city and cut off railroad supply lines from
Petersburg to the Confederate capital, Richmond.
The success of this mission was the final blow to the
Confederacy. Lee surrendered weeks later.

28 🛡 VA 95 MILE

Virginia is the most southern of the Middle Atlantic States.

One would think that the former capital of the Confederacy, where the Civil War is still referred to as the "War Between the States," would be lumped together with other Southern states. But, no. Geographically at least, Virginia is considered by most authorities to be part of the Middle Atlantic Region.

America's biggest, most audacious cattle raid happened here in Sussex County.

Confederate troops in Petersburg (about 20 miles north) were starving, cut off from supply lines during the Siege. A Confederate scout spotted a herd of about 3,000 cattle, destined to feed Union troops, just five miles from Lt. Gen. Grant's camp. Desperation led to a bold plan and 3,000 Southern

soldiers set out to rustle the whole herd. One of the great victories for the Confederate side, exactly 2,486 steer were herded into Petersburg on September 17, 1864.

It happened a few miles north of here. The soldiers drove the cattle across Nottoway River, which crosses under I-95 near MP 28.

Emporia

When little Emporia, with a population hovering around 6,000, hosts the annual Virginia Pork Festival, the number of people filling the streets swells to 15,000. It takes that many to chow down on the 20 tons of pork brought in for the festival.

That's in June but come September, get ready for the annual Great Peanut Bicycle Tour. "Only" 1,500 people show up for that annual 125-mile tour.

Smithfield Hams

One thing's for sure; there will be some Smithfield Ham at the Pork Festival. The town of Smithfield, Virginia (about 60 miles northeast of here) has a monopoly on Smithfield Ham. More accurately, since 1926 the only cured ham with the right to call itself Smithfield Ham, has to be made in Smithfield. The legacy goes back to 1779 when refrigeration was a thing of the future. To preserve pork, folks slathered it with salt and hung it out to dry for about three months. It worked! Smithfield perfected the process and now Smithfield Foods is a Fortune 500 mega-company.

Roanoke Rapids

① 95

②

Rocky Mount

Tarboro

③ Wilson

Lucama

Selma

Smithfield

Benson

Kenly

④

⑤

Fort Bragg ⑥

Fayetteville

Spivey's Corner

95

⑦ Tar Heel

Lumberton

Raleigh

85

40

40

Wilmington

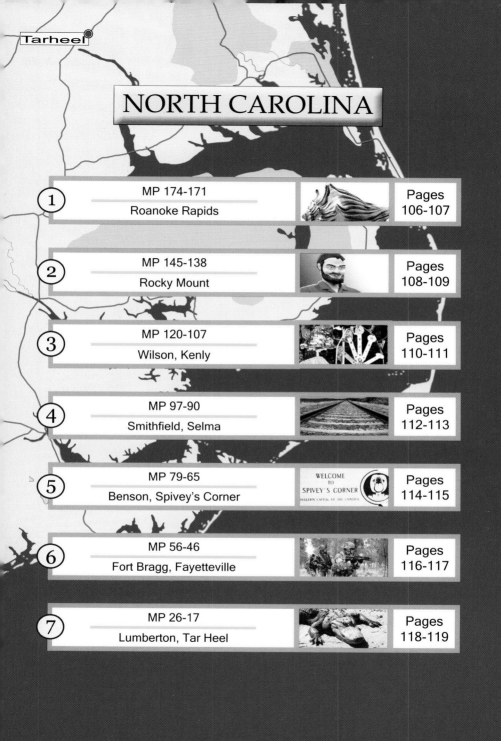

NORTH CAROLINA

WELCOME TO SPIVEY'S CORNER

Tarheel

The river determined the towns' locations.

Near MP 174, where I-95 crosses the river, catch a glimpse at the reason Weldon (to the east) and Roanoke Rapids (to the west) are located here. At the headwaters of the Roanoke River the setting was perfect for a new town or two. Water powered the mills and railroads delivering goods both inland and outbound for shipment.

Rockfish

Rockfish, otherwise known as striped bass, couldn't care less about that. They just want to get here to spawn in the headwaters by the first of April. It's not a sound plan as far as the fish are concerned because fishermen descend on this area each spring for the best Rockfish fishing in the country.

RoRap, as Roanoke Rapids is called, deserves its nickname "Rockfish Capital."

Roanoke, a name with a history.

The word Roanoke, according to most sources, meant money in the Algonquian language. The words peak, marginalia and minfel meant money too. They were all forms of wampum and were usually made from the Whelk shell (shown above) or Venus clam.

Black and purple beads were twice the value of white. Strung together by color, their value was measured by the length of one's arm.

Remember the 1979 movie *Norma Rae?*

Sally Fields won an academy award for her portrayal of a union sympathizer. Everyone loved her. The movie was based on the true-life story of Crystal Lee Sutton, a single mother who battled for the Union single-handed. It happened at the J.P. Stevens textile plant here in Roanoke Rapids. Everyone thought the victory of union workers over plant owners would revolutionize all unions in North Carolina. The truth is, even after that "win" it took the company six years to negotiate a contract.

This 1908 image of a child working in a South Carolina textile mill shows the desperate need for unions in those days.

Carolina Crossroads

In its infancy this dream looked something like a budding Branson, Missouri – a mushrooming network of lively theaters attracting local city folk and I-95 travelers to musical revues and other entertainment. No sense in pointing fingers, but the lonely building on the east side of the road at MP 171 is all that got past local politics and puffery. Eternally hopeful, taxpayers around here believe the next owner will pull the project out of the fire.

That real big guy, the one 40-feet tall, standing along the interstate at about MP 145 used to work as Stan the Tire Man in Illinois.

A few years ago he retired to the moderate climate of North Carolina.

Possibly the Paul Bunyon-esque, ax-wielding brute is happier overseeing the property of Original Log Cabin Homes. He does look at home here.

Burgers in Rocky Mount

North Carolina native, Wilbur Hardee dreamed of having his own restaurant. After some false starts, including the Do Drop Inn, he simplified things. No tables, no waiters, just a 15¢ hamburger plus a few odds and ends.

The name was nothing fancy either; he named it after himself. Just like that, investors approached him and, together, they opened the first Hardees's franchise in Rocky Mount. That was 1961 and that original restaurant is gone. Now there are nearly 2,000 Hardees restaurants; the closest one to I-95 is at Exit 145.

IBX - Vacation Destination

For years, the Outer Banks received all the glory. It seemed everyone was going to North Carolina's string of off shore islands.
Even the name is alluring - The Outer Banks.
As far as tourism officials were concerned, not enough vacationers thought to try other parts of North Carolina; they just didn't know all the great stuff to do and see there.

Tourism breeds creative solutions and the Inner Banks is one of them. It's a "new" region that is located generally from I-95 east until you get near the shore. Everything in the Coastal Plains Province not claimed by the Outer Banks is now the Inner Banks although coastal towns identify with the concept more than inland folks.

Local people rarely use the term (unless they're in the tourism business) but IBX is the cheeky shorthand for Inner Banks.

Morning sickness or sea sickness?

Eleanor Dare was pregnant when she boarded a ship in England, sailing to an unknown land across the Atlantic Ocean. She was one month from giving birth when they landed on Roanoke Island, about 125 miles east of this spot on I-95.

The baby, Virginia Dare, arrived on August 18, 1587. She was the first English child born in the New World. Ten days later, the group's leader (John While, Eleanor's father) left for England to get supplies.

Delayed for three years, when he finally returned he found a mystery that endures today. All of the colonists were gone.

There were not enough clues to piece together the fate of the settlers.
To this day, the Lost Colony represents the ultimate "cold case."

Raleigh, the state capital

Sir Walter Raleigh, in an effort to colonize the New World, sent the doomed Lost Colony across the ocean to Roanoke Island. He is honored with the name of the capital of North Carolina, which is 35 miles east of MP 119.

Wilson

The water tower at MP 120 proudly advertises the town of Wilson. It is known as one of North Carolina's most beautiful cities but has also earned other nicknames: City of Beautiful Trees, City of Antiques and America's Largest Tobacco Market (when it boasted the world's largest bright leaf tobacco market). You might not see it while zipping by on the interstate, but the water tower also mentions another big accomplishment for the town: The National Civic League bestowed the honor of All-American City on Wilson twice.

The National Civic League has been recognizing effective political and community leadership with the All-American City Award since 1949. All cities have challenges but the NCL honors those who tackle them and achieve results.

World Famous Whirligigs

One look at the intricate moveable art at Vollis Simpson's place in a tiny community of Lucama, you know someone special created these pieces with love – and lots of junk. He will use anything: old gears, discarded license plates, even the kitchen sink if he can figure out how to make it twirl around. It's a hobby for this aging artist (his 2011 Facebook page says he was born in 1919 and still going strong) but this hobby has attracted national attention.

Newsweek, Time, PBS, the Carolina Museum of Art and the 1996 Olympics in Atlanta have all featured Vollis and his creations, which are each born strictly from his own self-taught imagination.

Because North Carolina grows more sweet potatoes than any other state, the Wilson County students petitioned the government to officially make the tuber the state vegetable. Since 1995, it has had that honor.

Tobacco Farm Life Museum

Much of this state was built on tobacco. The sandy soil in the Coastal Plains is especially suited to the crop. The families around here who grew up working in the business are proud of their heritage. They started a museum, really more like a historical tobacco community, to demonstrate that slow, Southern lifestyle. If you go, you'll come away knowing the hard but happy life of a Depression era tobacco farm. And you'll get to see one of Vollis' whirligigs; the one pictured above is located at the entry to the museum in Kenly at Exit 107.

Signs along the interstate mention "Historic Union Station," referring to the 1924 restored train station that now greets passengers on the Amtrak line. Several railroad tracks, on the way there, gather under the overpass at Exit 98.

Spook Joyner, Selma's Showman

After 40 years of hanging on in the competitive music business, Spook Joyner realized his dream. Demonstrating his showmanship as a talented writer, promoter and director, Spook is the master of ceremonies at Rudy Theater in Selma, NC. He isn't all show, though. He cares about his community. Working with the North Carolina school system, Spook put together a funny but educational show (don't tell the kids) that reinforces teachers' lessons. He charges students all of $8 a show. Teachers; no charge. And, he throws a bit of magic in – drinks and popcorn are free!

JR's Tobacco Shop

Long the king of tacky billboards, South of the Border has competition. JR Cigar Store (Exit 97) sells itself as the largest cigar store in the world but they are so much more that. On a recent visit, discount wedding dresses dominated the floor near the entrance. When asked where the bathrooms were, a friendly employee cheerfully said, "By the big yellow sign back by the flamingoes." Enough said.

The Battle of Bentonville

Signs along the interstate let you know that Exit 90 leads to Bentonville Civil War Battleground but it doesn't tell you that on March 19,1865 over 80,000 men prepared for one of the Civil War's final battles. By the end of the three-day battle, 433 soldiers were dead and the Union again had shown their superior strength.

The Hardee Hat, sometimes called the Jeff Davis Hat, was distinctive head wear approved for the entire Confederate army. The golden eagle on one side was counterbalanced with an ostrich feather on the other. The horn on the front represented the infantry.

A starlet from Smithfield (Exit 95)

Old Hollywood buffs might like to know that Ava Gardner, sexy film star of the mid-1900's, was born near Smithfield. There's a museum here that chronicles her life.

At the age of 18, she went to New York City to visit her sister and brother-in-law, a professional photographer. He snapped some pictures of Ava and displayed them in the window of his Fifth Avenue shop. Her stunning beauty caught the eye of a passer-by who said something like, "That girl should be in pictures!"

By the close of that year, 1941, she had a contract with MGM.

79 ⬤ NC 95 MILE

From I-95 you'd never guess that this corner of
North Carolina is a hotbed of fun.
Three major festivals occur annually within a few miles of here.

For at least 60 years Benson (Exit 79) has celebrated Mule Days. Each September people gather for rodeos, mule-pulling contests and bluegrass music. Attracting up to 70,000, it's one of North Carolina's biggest festivals.

That's not all.

Nearly 90 years ago some folks in Benson were proud enough of their singing that they invited a crowd of 200 people to gather in the local tobacco warehouse to hear some good old southern gospel songs. That turned into a yearly event and now it's called the Benson Singing Convention. The nation's oldest southern gospel singing convention attracts 50 professional and semi-professional groups in a joyous three-day outdoor celebration.

The welcome sign for Spivey's Corner is a scream!

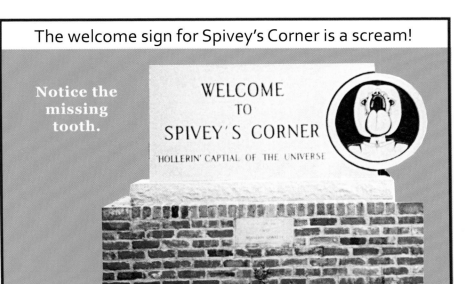

Notice the missing tooth.

WELCOME
TO
SPIVEY'S CORNER
'HOLLERIN' CAPTIAL OF THE UNIVERSE

About ten miles directly east of MP 65 is the site of the National Hollerin' Contest in Spivey's Corner. That's out of hollerin' range from the interstate. A good hefty holler travels up to three miles. But if you got all attendees hollerin' at once (up to 10,000 people descend on Spivey's Corner the third Saturday of June), you might get an earful.

Contestants compete in four categories: distress, pleasure, functional and communicative. Participants consider this to be a serious art form, which has been featured on The Tonight Show and in Sports Illustrated.

If you don't feel like hollerin', there's a Conch Shell Blowin' contest too.

Fort Bragg

This is the "Home of the Airborne and Special Operations Forces" training the 82nd Airborne Division to deploy within eighteen hours to anywhere in the world.
Modern Minutemen.

Three museums on Fort Bragg property explain the mission and, as it says on the web site, hours are "1000 to 1600 hours, Tuesday through Sunday."
If you go, listen for a hearty "HOOAH" from a soldier. It's the traditional greeting that expresses everything from "We're ready for action" to "Great job!"

No wonder this area is famous for its golf courses.

North Carolina's natural sand traps were 20 million years in the making. The level of the ocean was 300 feet higher then than it is today. The water's edge, in the Miocene Epoch, was just west of today's interstate. When the water receded, the sandy beach and near-shore ocean bottom were left high and dry. You can see the remnants of those days particularly in the medial strip near MP 47. Notice how sand often peaks through the thin grasses.

Could that beach have resembled Edgar Degas' painting?

Cape Fear River

Cape Fear and the Cape Fear River have appeared on maps as far back as 1585. You might be able to tell as you cross over it near MP 46 that it's a blackwater river, a slow moving, lazy river stained by decaying plants. It's nature's tea bag, in a way. Blackwater rivers occur in two major places in the world: the southern United States and the Amazon.

This little critter loves these waters. The Cape Fear Shiner lives nowhere else in the world.

A varmint of another sort also frequented the Cape Fear waters. Pirates found this river, and other shallow inlets in the Outer Banks, to be a haven from the law.

Tar Heel

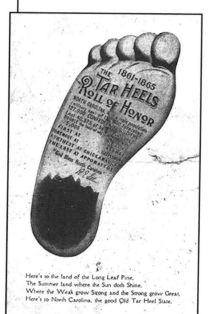

There's Tarheel, Tar Heel and Tarboro – all North Carolina communities. And, if you didn't know it, this is the Tar Heel State. No one knows for sure why or how it acquired the nickname but the most popular explanation is North Carolinians' tenacity during the Civil War; they stuck in a battle like there was tar on their heels.

They paid dearly for that honor.

Historians acknowledge record keeping was poor but statistics from the war still show startling numbers. North Carolina sacrificed 20,602 of her men in the War Between the States, dead or wounded. That's nearly three times the loss of Virginia, the state with the next heaviest casualties.

At Gettysburg one North Carolinian regiment lost 714 of its 800 men; 584 on the first day.

Tar, pitch and turpentine were products derived from North Carolina's abundant pine forest. It is fitting, then, that the pine tree is their official state tree. No specific species was singled out but the Loblolly (seen here) is the most common of the eight types indigenous to the state.

Pine tree by-products helped establish this area's importance during colonial times. Tar, pitch and turpentine, vital to the British navy for treating their ships' hulls, were collectively known as naval stores. That, along with the lumber itself, was one of the Carolina's major products and exports.

You might look differently on all those trees along the interstate now that you know the rest of the story.

GATORS!

Alligators are known to live as far north as Nag's Head but they don't venture inland unless they are in a warmer climate. Here at the southernmost part of North Carolina, alligators thrive as far inland as I-95. They love the swampy Cape Fear River Basin. Since they don't eat unless the mercury rises above 70°, North Carolina gators are smaller than those that live farther south.

Venus Flytrap

A lot of kids attempt to grow the awesome Venus Flytrap, that carnivorous plant that snaps its jaws shut at the mere tickle from a fly's movement. The plant is grown in greenhouses all over the world. But it is native only to one place and that is within a 100-mile radius of Wilmington, North Carolina, well within the reach of I-95.

INTERESTING INTERSTATES

SOUTH CAROLINA

SOUTHERN HOSPITALITY AT ITS FINEST

An abundance of palm trees frame the I-95 portals to South Carolina, both north and south. More than a beautiful welcome, it is steeped in history and meaning.

First of all, it represents warm weather to road weary travelers. Sabal palms tolerate freezing temperatures but they look so - well, tropical.

The sabal palm is on the state flag. It's on the license plates and proudly displayed on nearly everything referring to South Carolina.

Why?

During the Revolutionary War, Colonel William Moultrie defended the colonies from British attack from behind the walls of a fort made of sabal palm logs. Cannon balls fired at the fort didn't penetrate the walls. Instead they became embedded in the spongy wood, which saved the day for the colonists.

This symbol of tenacity became the state tree.

For 38 years, a confederate flag flew over the state capitol building until it was replaced on July 1, 2000 by the state flag shown above. Only on Confederate Memorial Day, May 1st, is the Battle Flag of Confederate States of America allowed to fly over the capital.

POST 193

Once upon a time Al Schafer had a little wine and beer store in North Carolina. But when the county where his business was located went dry - no more alcohol.

He solved the problem by moving his business over the border into Dillon, South Carolina about 60 years ago.

The name change to reflect the new location led to a theme;

South of the Border = Mexico.

Supplementing the liquor business, Al sold Mexican trinkets, a gimmick that caused his business to grow and grow. Now it's a theme park of sorts and, no matter how kitschy, a must-stop for many interstate travelers.

Up to 250 clever billboards used to line the route from Philadelphia to Daytona but ol' Pedro has scaled back. Now there are fewer signs in fewer states. They are more politically correct – and not nearly as entertaining as they used to be. But they still get a boatload of motorists to stop at the 200-foot tall Sombrero Tower.

BLACK HAWK DOWN !

Rainy and dark - perfect conditions for a routine nighttime training mission using night-vision goggles. Or so it seemed in April 2004.

That night soldiers took off from Fort Bragg for the mission in two Black Hawk helicopters but only one returned. The other, with three soldiers aboard, went down in the heavy underbrush you see along the interstate.

Despite using radar and heat-seeking equipment, no one could find the chopper - not until a trucker on I-95, right about at MP 175, noticed a wheel in the median strip and some trees that were recently lopped off. The Black Hawk crashed just north of the Pee Dee River and virtually disappeared 30-feet below I-95.

As you cross over the scenic Great Pee Dee River at MP 175, try humming the Stephen Foster favorite *Way Down Upon the Swanee River*.

When he wrote the song in 1851, Foster first used Mississippi's Yazoo River in the lyrics but it didn't have the right sound.

Then he changed it to Way Down Upon the Pee Dee River.

That name wasn't perfect enough to make the cut.

Foster's brother, according to legend, scoured a map to come up with a more lyrical name. Suwannee had a melodious lilt to it and, though Foster misspelled it in the written version, that's the name that stuck.

POST 164

Harold Brasington embodies persistence and the importance of following your dream.
His dream, Darlington Raceway, is near I-95 at Exit 164.

He loved car racing and, in 1933, attended the granddaddy event, the Indianapolis 500. Why couldn't he build his own track right in his hometown of Darlington, he wondered. By 1949 bulldozers were scraping out a track from an old peanut field. "Harold's Folly," as the local folks called it, was taking shape. But it had an odd shape. There was a fishing hole on the property and the track veered around it, creating an egg shape rather than the traditional oval. But the question remained – would this be a success? On Labor Day, 1950, Brasington hoped to attract 10,000 fans to the first race. He was astounded when 25,000 showed up. For sixty-plus years, this impossible dream of Harold Brasington has attracted all the top names of stock car racing including Dale Earnhardt, David Pearson and Richard Petty.

As many as 63,000 fans can fit into Darlington's stands.

Quick! What's the capital of South Carolina?
It's Columbia, which is about 60 miles directly west of here.

Fort Sumter, about 100 miles east of here in the Charleston harbor, took the first shots of the Civil War on April 12, 1861. The town of Sumter, about 17 miles east of here, experienced almost a mirror image of the conflict.

When General Robert E. Lee surrendered on April 9, 1865, the war was over. But leaders in the field hadn't heard the news.

Brigadier General Edward E. Potter, for instance, marched 2,700 men through this area, burning nearly anything they could find – mills, trains, cotton, houses. On the very day the war was declared over, 575 men from Sumter gathered to defend what was left. Many of them died in the effort.

Here's an excerpt from a letter written by a Union soldier after Potter's Raid.

"...the rebels stood for the last time; for we slaughtered them in great numbers. They left the field strewn with their dead and wounded. We captured ... fifteen locomotives, and one hundred and forty cars loaded with ammunition, small arms and stores. We destroyed them all. We captured five hundred contrabands, five hundred prisoners, destroyed a vast deal of property, and captured about eighty head of horses."

Both the fort and the town are named after General Sumter who made a name for himself in the Revolutionary War. His nickname was the "Fighting Gamecock" for a bird bred to fight to the death in cockfights - they just won't give up.

It's a handsome fowl with garnet and black feathers and, not coincidentally, those are the colors of the University of South Carolina's athletic teams. College kids, no doubt, have a lot of fun with the mascot's name – Cocky.

MORE BIRDS!

In the 1920's, Hamilton Bland tried planting some Japanese irises to spice up his private fishing lake but it was a dismal failure. He had them dug up and dumped in the swamp. Ah, that's just what they were waiting for! The next year they bloomed exuberantly and that was the start of a lovely botanical garden that is complete, these days, with all eight varieties of swans.

Memorial Day weekend is the time to visit; that's when the Swan Lake and Iris Gardens in Sumter hosts an Iris Festival.

Remember childhood stories about Amelia Bedelia?

In a way, she was born right here in Manning at Exit 119. Peggy Parish, a Manning native, conceived of the light-hearted stories about a very literal housekeeper from some of her own family experiences.

THE SWAMP FOX

At MP 115 you are driving through Clarendon County where the British waged battles during the American Revolution.

The swampy floor seen along the shoulder of the interstate shows what this area was like in the 18th century. Not pleasant or easily negotiated.

During the war, the colonists fought back but their chance of success looked bleak. It took a special character to turn the tide. General Francis Marion had learned a trick or two while fighting the Cherokee Indians years before and knew how to use this landscape as an advantage rather than a detriment. He saved the day by successfully outwitting the British troops and that earned him the nickname The Swamp Fox.

Today he is honored with a series of building-sized murals in four towns (Paxville, Summerton, Turbeville and Manning) that define the area the Swamp Fox dominated. Each scene tells a story of South Carolina during the Revolutionary War but none can be seen from the interstate.

POST ⑨⑤ 100

The area's Native Americans were the Santee Indians, part of the Sioux culture.

The territory of this small tribe centered right here in Clarendon, Orangeburg and Calhoun Counties. According to tribal ways, when a loved one died they built a mound and laid the body on top during a period of mourning. In fact I-95 comes within one mile (at MP 102) of one of their ceremonial burial mounds, shown here.

During the Revolutionary War, the British built a fort on top of the mound, which served as a great lookout and aerial vantage point for sniping at the colonial soldiers.

Colonel Marion, The Swamp Fox, wasn't deterred. He simply built a tower taller than the fort and fired in at the British, who gave up after eight days.

As you cross the 4-mile stretch of Lake Marion (named, of course, for General Marion) consider this: when this land was flooded in the 1940's as part of a hydroelectric project, Marion's childhood home (along with other small communities) was engulfed by the lake.

Charleston

After its founding in 1670, Charleston endured six hurricanes, the first major naval battle of the Revolutionary War, a two-and-a-half year occupation by British troops, the first shots of the Civil War and, in the final throws of that war, devastating fires throughout the city. But it was a freak earthquake in 1886 that laid the town to waste.

Between 6.9 and 7.3 on the Richter scale, it was the biggest earthquake to ever hit the eastern United States. Over $6 million dollars in damage was recorded in a city with property valued at only $24 million. Over 90% of the buildings were damaged. Between 60 and 110 people died.

As odd as it seems, over 30 earthquakes have been recorded in the Charleston area since 1974. In 2007 the South Carolina Earthquake Education and Preparedness Program was set up in the College of Charleston campus to study the issue.

Poinsettias

In 1826, the United States' ambassador to Mexico, who was a curious amateur botanist, took time during a diplomatic mission to search the Mexican countryside for unique specimens. He found an enthralling native plant called *Euphorbia pulcherrima* that appeared to have brilliant red flowers.

The ambassador, Joel Poinsett, had never seen anything like it around his hometown of Charleston. The cuttings he took home to his greenhouse soon multiplied and within a few short years it became a hugely popular potted plant.

When a historian/botanist was asked to assign a common name to the plant, he chose "Poinsettia" to honor the man responsible for bringing it to the US.

Even Montezuma, the Aztec king, coveted the "Mexican fire plant."

Rumors circulated for years that the beautiful Poinsettia plant was terribly poisonous but a study at Ohio State University proved that to be false. Other than irritated skin from the milky sap or an upset tummy from gulping down a bushel of leaves, the plant is innocuous.

Most towns near here got their start because either a river or a railroad ran through the area. For **Walterboro**, it was mosquitoes.

Two brothers, Paul and Jacob Walter, were rice planters working and living on the coast. Paul's daughter came down with malaria, a common problem in the mosquito-infested swamps of the Lowcountry.

Looking for higher ground for a summer retreat, they found it here and established a community called Walterborough, since shortened to Walterboro.

Higher ground or not, if you get off the interstate here in the summer, you'll immediately feel what "sultry" is all about. Hot and humid is an understatement.

And they didn't really get away from the swamps either. In fact, the Great Swamp Sanctuary is in the city limits, about 1.5 miles from the interstate at Exit 57. A wagon road used for commerce between Charleston and Savannah ran right through the swamp – and still does. It's part of a network of trails now used for hiking and biking through America's only braided creek that is accessible to the public.

A braided creek has no defined waterway but, instead, several meandering channels.

PEACHES

California may grow more peaches but South Carolina, with the second biggest crop in the country, prefers to think of themselves as the "Tastier Peach State."

Sorry Georgia, but even though you are officially known as the "Peach State," you come in at #3 in total production. With 30 – 40 varieties of peaches grown here, South Carolina's state fruit is harvested from May through September.

They've had a lot of practice too; South Carolina peaches have been shipped north commercially since the mid-1800's.

Wright, perhaps America's best-known architect, designed over 1,000 buildings but only one plantation. It's called Auldbrass and is less than four miles from the interstate near MP 38. But don't expect to find stately columns and antebellum doodads. This plantation is as sleek as his other designs, conforming to the lean of the live oaks found on the property.

It has struggled over the years, enduring several owners and years of neglect. But true love won out. In 1987, Joel Silver bought the place. He is best known as a film director (think Matrix and Die Hard) but his heart belongs to Frank.

If Frank were alive, he'd no doubt feel quite fond of Joel too because he has faithfully restored Auldbrass to its original design. In accordance with the purchase agreement, Silver opens his private home to the public one day every two years.

THE CHEROKEE PLANTATION NEAR MP 38

You'd never believe that just a couple of miles beyond the thick trees along the interstate there is one of the most exclusive private clubs in America. Once a rice plantation called The Boardhouse, in the 1930's it took a much more romantic sounding name, Cherokee Plantation from the ubiquitous Cherokee Rose.

One owner of the plantation was Robert Beverly Evans, president of American Motors, which was about to roll out a new style of Jeep. It needed a catchy name and Evans looked to his beloved plantation and called it the Jeep Cherokee.

Then in 1999, magic started to happen; the old place was transformed into a billionaire's dream. A one million dollar initiation fee, if you are one of the lucky 25 accepted for membership, gets you in the front door and access to a golf course, spa, great fishing holes, etc. The $85,000 yearly dues keep you there.

CHEROKEE ROSE

The Cherokee Rose is a tenacious climbing rose that is native to China but, since its introduction to America in the 1780's, has become naturalized in southeastern United States.

HAROLD'S COUNTRY CLUB NEAR MP 33

From the opulence of Cherokee Plantation, we slide down to the other end of the "Southern elegance" meter to find Harold's Country Club. This restaurant/gas station/pool room/fish bait shop pulls in clients from nearby fields and Hollywood stage sets.

You call for reservations (reserving food, not a table) for burgers on Wednesday, pot luck on Thursday or steak on Saturday.

After dinner, join in with the karaoke.

And if you need to gas up the car before leaving, you'll have to remember some simple math: the antique gas pumps go only as high as $1.60 per gallon. These days you have to double it (at least) and adjust from there.

Juanita White Crosswalk near MP 19

The community of Mitchellville was cut in two with the construction of I-95 in the early 1970's. Ten years later this impressive crosswalk was erected to ferry pedestrians safely to the other side of the road. Juanita M. White, a State Representative for District 122, was honored as the crosswalk was named after her.

There's no Matterhorn around here but Exit 18 southbound lists Switzerland on the exit sign.

That might seem unlikely but it's not and here's why. Jean Pierre Purry, a tenacious fellow from Switzerland, believed ideal living conditions were found at 33° latitude. To him it didn't matter if it was north or south. First he chose south, trying unsuccessfully to convince financial backers to send a slew of his fellow Swiss to southern Australia. But in 1730, the colonial government wanted settlers to move to the Carolina coast, offering enticements like transportation, a year's worth of provisions and free land. It happened to be near 33° latitude north. Perfect.

Almost.

Purry, with many Swiss families, sailed the Atlantic to a 20,000-acre tract of land that included this area that I-95 goes through today. The town was called Purrysburgh but it didn't last long. Malaria took its toll. So did the infertile soil; it couldn't support crops to sustain a town. Although the residents dispersed to other thriving towns, today's little community of Switzerland lies in the heart of the Purrysburgh land grant.

South Carolina's official magazine is called the Sandlapper.

It's a distinctive name to be sure but even South Carolinians themselves can't agree on the origin of the name. Historians came up with the likeliest explanation.

It has to do with eating dirt, or a practice called geophagia.

In many places, the state's sand hills are mixed with a mineral called kaolin. That's the stomach-soothing ingredient in Kaopectate.

In the past there were reports that many people were seen eating the dirt, perhaps a practice that came to America with the slave trade. As part of their traditional medicine, this was one of the methods handed down through the generations.

It was a jarring sight to visitors and they coined the term "Sandlappers," "Sandhillers" and "Carolina Clay-Eaters."

Like North Carolina's Tar Heels, they now wear the nickname with pride.

Hardeeville once supported one of the largest lumber operations in the world, as you might guess from the oppressive tunnel of trees squeezing in around the interstate near MP 5 .

But Hardeeville's strategic position along the Savannah-Charleston railroad line helped send it into the history books.

During the Civil War, Union troops sought to cut the railroad tracks between the two important coastal cities, shutting down both communications and supplies. When the 5,000 soldiers marched up this way to Honey Hill (less than a mile from Exit 21), they were surprised by a forceful showing of 1,400 Confederate soldiers. The Rebels drove them back and saved the railroad.

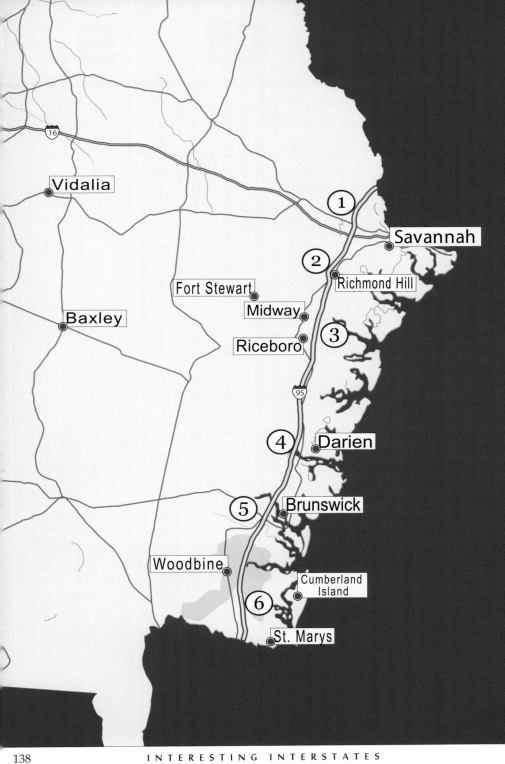

Vidalia

Savannah

Richmond Hill

Fort Stewart

Midway

Baxley

Riceboro

Darien

Brunswick

Woodbine

Cumberland Island

St. Marys

GEORGIA

1 MP 109-102
Vidalia, Plains

Pages 140-141

2 MP 99-90
Richmond Hill, Savannah

Pages 142-143

3 MP 76-73
Midway, Liberty County

Pages 145-146

4 MP 49-46
Darien, Butler Island

Pages 147-148

5 MP 34-31
Brunswick

Pages 149-150

6 MP 14-3
Woodbine, St. Marys

Pages 151-152

Nearly every interchange, viaduct and stretch of highway in Georgia is named for someone. Exit 109 is no exception but the man it's named after, Christmas Moultrie, is different. He was a slave, born on Mulberry Plantation on Christmas Day in 1863. After the abolition of slavery, he remained on Mulberry Plantation (which grazes I-95 near here) and became an accomplished market hunter, a hunter with the cunning and determination to make a living tracking and selling birds and game.

A vibrant Jimmy Carter in 2008.

Even if you look hard you'll probably miss the view of the railroad tracks shooting beneath the interstate near MP 101. They look like any other track but this one runs the SAM Short Line, an excursion train based west of here in Cordele.

So what, you say?

Well, occasionally it heads farther west to Plains, Georgia where President Jimmy Carter lives. On his birthday, February 16th, President Carter personally greets SAM passengers at his alma mater, Plains High School. That's nearly 200 miles from here. Rarely does the tourist train zip under I-95 on its way to Savannah, but sometimes it does. After all, SAM stands for Savannah-Americus-Montgomery.

Vidalia Onion Festival

No one knew exactly why, but in 1931 Mose Coleman, a farmer located about 70 miles west of MP 102, found that his onions were sweeter than all others. By the 1970's they were marketed all over the nation. They were named for Mose's hometown of Vidalia.

Many farmers tried to capitalize on his success, trying to pass their own (inferior) onions off as Vidalias.

This spurred the Vidalia Onion Act of 1986. Now, by official federal order, the onion is safely protected; to be a Vidalia it has to be grown in a 20-county radius near the original farm. No other onion can call itself Vidalia.

Every May, the SAM Short Line takes visitors to the Vidalia Onion Festival to enjoy a rodeo, motorcycle rally, air show, an Onion Run and Miss Vidalia Onion Pageant.

Mighty Eighth Air Force Museum near MP 102

That B-47 Stratojet along the interstate just north of Exit 102 was once used in the fight against the Soviet nuclear threat. It now rests in the Memorial Garden of the Mighty Eighth Air Force Museum. The Eighth Air Force first showed their valor against Nazi Germany during WWII. They still serve as a superior strike element in today's conflicts. The museum highlights the considerable sacrifices these dedicated men and women have made to help keep our country safe.

You'll be forgiven for humming "Tara's Theme" from the *Gone With the Wind* as you drive through this area.

SAVANNAH

After William Tecumseh Sherman ravaged Atlanta (as depicted in the movie) he set his sights on Savannah. Death and destruction didn't seem to worry him on the way here but when he saw the beauty of Savannah, he stopped.

He couldn't destroy it.

Instead, after capturing the city on December 21, 1864, he offered it as a Christmas gift to President Lincoln.

This fountain in Savannah's Forsyth Park was added in 1858. Perhaps it helped inspire that gift to Abraham Lincoln.

A Cinderella story in Richmond Hill at Exit 90.

Surrounding communities were not as lucky as Savannah. With the burning of their buildings, hope and prosperity went up in smoke too. For sixty years, the area's residents languished in poverty.

Then, in 1925, a couple came to town looking for a summer retreat. No doubt they were driving a Ford.

Henry Ford, whose fortune flourished with the auto industry, bought the old Richmond Plantation that was destroyed during the Civil War. Not only did he build a house for himself and his wife, but over the next 22 years, he also constructed a mill, a church and schools. Ford drained the swamps to control malaria, subsidized health care, employed 600 area residents and built houses for them too.

Single-handedly, he pulled Richmond Hill out of despair in into prosperity once again.

The magic didn't stop there.

When the government was looking for a home for the 3rd Infantry Division, they knew they needed a lot of land for an anti-aircraft artillery-training center. They found it here.

Fort Stewart (also at Exit 90) is the largest military installation east of the Mississippi and it's getting bigger. To bring in the 5th Brigade Combat Team by 2011, $400 million in new on-base projects are in the works. That is boosting the economy for the whole area.

Midway at MP 76

Midway is halfway between Charleston, SC and Jacksonville, FL but that's just by chance. Midway got its name from the Midway Society, a Congregationalist group that moved here from South Carolina in the mid-1700's.

If it's actively spewing out steam, the Edwin I. Hatch Nuclear Power Plant near Baxley is easy to see from the top of the overpass at MP 73.
You might not guess that it is about 60 miles west of the interstate.

There is one other nuclear plant in Georgia and together they produce one-fourth of the state's electricity output.

The other plant, Vogtle Nuclear Power Plant near Augusta, was built in 1983. During excavation, they found something truly remarkable; the largest whale fossil ever found. The skeleton was about 11 feet long and the skull measured three feet from front to back. (How does that compare to your car's dimensions?)
The Georgiacetus vogtlensis, as it was named, had four well-developed legs.

Remember – Augusta is about 100 miles from today's shoreline!

Georgia On My Mind

When Hoagy Carmichael picked out a tune in 1930, he didn't know it would become the state song of Georgia. Stuart Gorrell added lyrics, which were written about Hoagy's sister, and still neither of them could have guessed that almost 50 years later Georgia On My Mind would come to define the heart and soul of the state. Ray Charles' passionate rendition in 1960, charged with emotion, brought the song nationwide attention. It is a perfect song to reflect Georgia's southern charm.

Product of the area's extensive rice fields.

Signs along I-95 close to Exit 76 mention the

Historic Liberty Trail.

Liberty refers to the county and the 10-stop trail highlights the county's treasures. Besides relics of the Revolutionary and Civil Wars, lush natural preserves and a nod to the area's history of rice cultivation, one of the most unique elements of the car tour is the Geechee Kunda Cultural Arts Center.

In the Carolinas they are known as Gullah, but called Geechee in Georgia and northern Florida. Together they are a distinct group of African Americans with a common history of slavery mixed with a colonial way of life. This group is so culturally unique, the federal government designated this entire coastal area the Gullah/Geechee Cultural Heritage Corridor.

Fort King George at Exit 49 served the Brits for only six years and saw little action during that time. It must have been a lonely assignment to guard Britain's southernmost outpost.

Bagpipes? Really?

Around the same time the fort was built (1735), 170 Scottish Highlanders settled here, founding the town of Darien. Their heritage influenced Georgia's culture. Even today bagpipes are heard echoing over McIntosh County and at the occasional Scottish ceilidh (a traditional social gathering).

Darien's history of boom and bust is different from most other southern towns. Almost from the start, Darien's star shined bright.

The Altamaha River, at Darien's front door, was a natural roadway to the interior. Inland cotton plantations and lumber mills floated their products to the busy port at Darien (third only to Savannah and Charleston).

The marshes, which reached 30 miles inland, were blessed with a natural daily cleansing as the tides swelled and receded – the perfect situation for rice cultivation.

Their blessing did them in. While other towns fought for a railroad stop in their communities, Darien did just fine with the river, thank you. But soon cotton and lumber were moved by rail to Savannah, not by boat to Darien. Banks failed, the economy faltered. That was in the mid-1800's, before the Civil War.

Talk about a fish out of water!

Fannie Kemble was a talented English actress who fell for a Georgian plantation owner.

When Fannie and Pierce Butler married in 1834, he didn't own slaves but soon afterwards, he inherited a whole plantation full. The newlyweds moved to the plantation on Butler Island, which is less than one mile directly east of I-95 at MP 46. Much of the land you see on the horizon was part of his rice operation.

Trouble surfaced almost immediately; Pierce tried to convince Fannie that owning slaves was a good thing. It wasn't an easy sell: the outspoken Fannie tried to persuade him to emancipate his slaves.

This is all that remains of the original plantation.

After their divorce, she turned the tale of her married life, isolated in these swampy rice fields, seeing unbelievable human cruelty exacted on the slaves, into a published work titled *Journal of a Residence on a Georgian Plantation.* It was widely read in her home country of England. That, in part, is why the Parliament refused to support the Confederacy during the American Civil War.

Butler Island's Second Life.

Colonel T.L Huston, part owner of the New York Yankees, bought the island in 1925 and built a two-story brick house that sometimes hosted Babe Ruth. It is still there along with the ruins of Pierce Butler's old rice mill.

Brunswick
At only ten feet above sea level, it is Georgia's lowest-lying city.
Everyone pays attention when a storm like this one rolls in across the flat marshland.

Have you ever heard of Brunswick stew? Guess where it originated.

Don't be so quick to answer.

There's competition.

True, Brunswick, Georgia claims to have been the first to make the slow-cooked treat of meat, tomatoes, corn and (sometimes) okra and other goodies. But Brunswick County, Virginia also stakes that claim. That's where Mrs. Fearnow made this stew on Hope Farm.

POST 31

They are grinding up trees to make pulp and paper at the
Brunswick Cellulose plant seen near MP 33.

Before the soaring Sidney Lanier Bridge (seen in the distance behind the plant)
was constructed in 2003, Highway 17 traffic often had to stop and wait for ships
to cross beneath it on the Brunswick River.
Those struts, seen from I-95 at about MP 31, reach 480 feet in the air.

This is Sidney Lanier, an admired
and prolific poet.

After contracting tuberculosis,
he moved to Brunswick for the
favorable weather. That was at
the end of the Civil War.

While here, he found inspiration
in the expansive salt marshes
and wrote the popular poem "The
Marshes of Glynn," referring to
the county you are driving through.

The fun times roll at the Woodbine Opry at Exit 14.

The Woodbine Opry in Woodbine, Georgia invites local folks and friendly strangers to gather 'round for some blue grass, gospel or country music, depending on if it's Friday or Saturday.

Their web site encourages you to bring your own instrument (even if it's just your voice) to join in the good time.

You would think that unspoiled Cumberland Island with its wild horses and dripping Spanish moss, would be enough to lure visitors.

For Thomas Carnegie, brother of industrialist Andrew Carnegie, it was.

When snubbed by the few wealthy residents in the late 19th century, he simply bought a chunk of the island.

But the island has another claim to fame.

John F. Kennedy Jr. and Carolyn Bessette escaped to the relative seclusion of Cumberland Island to be married in 1996.

"St. Marys, at MP 3, is the second oldest continually inhabited city in the United States after St. Augustine, Florida. The city was first settled in the mid 1500s by the Spanish."

Georgia is called the Peach State but farmers here excel in pecans.

The yield is higher than in any other state but there's more to the story than that.

A highway marker in St. Marys (less than 10 miles from the interstate) makes a romantic claim; "First Pecan Trees Grown Here About 1840." The sign goes on to say that Captain Sam Flood found a pecan nut floating at sea. His wife planted it here in St. Marys. The tree flourished, producing a heavy crop of meaty nuts. Saplings from those first trees, the sign says, were distributed throughout the southeastern US.

Production rates are higher than any other state. The yield is not only higher but it's earlier too; each year the mild climate helps get pecans to market before the competitors'.

According to the Georgia Pecan Commission, pecans are the only nut trees native to the United States and were used as a food source for Native Americans throughout the Mississippi Valley.

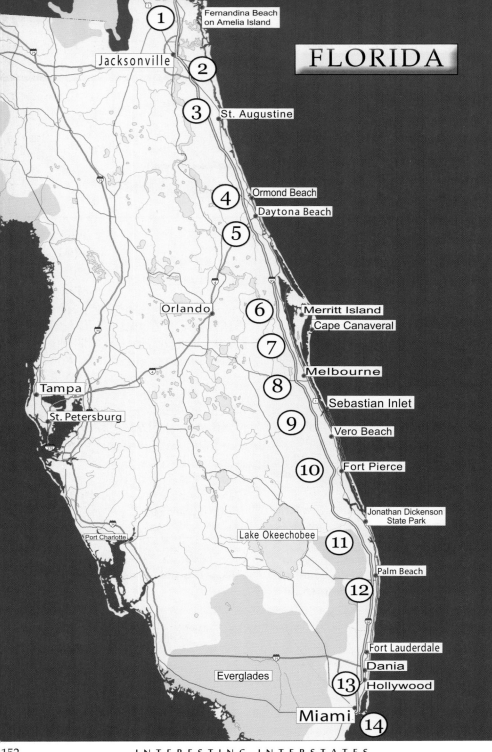

FLORIDA

1 — Fernandina Beach on Amelia Island

Jacksonville

2

3 — St. Augustine

4 — Ormond Beach

Daytona Beach

5

Orlando

6 — Merritt Island
Cape Canaveral

7

Tampa

8 — Melbourne

St. Petersburg

Sebastian Inlet

9 — Vero Beach

10 — Fort Pierce

Port Charlotte

Jonathan Dickenson State Park

Lake Okeechobee

11

Palm Beach

12

Fort Lauderdale

Everglades

Dania

13 — Hollywood

Miami 14

381 🛡️FL 95 MILE

The Agricultural Inspection Station near MP 381 is a sophisticated operation manned by highly-trained officers of the government.

But it wasn't always like that.

When the service started in 1935, sometimes local farmers were called into duty. These "road guards," as they were called, used flashlights to flag down vehicles while checking for compliance with the strict standards of the Florida Citrus Commission.

Things are different now. Well over 200 professional Agricultural Law Enforcement Officers staff 23 stations along the Florida border.

This station is concerned primarily with what comes into the state: any plant material or meat that might transport diseases into the state's farming community, whether it's citrus, livestock, aquaculture or horticulture, could be disastrous to the economy.

An industry worth $62 billion to is worth protecting.

Turtle hatchlings are driven by instinct to crawl toward the light of a breaking day, finding their way to the ocean. This worked fine before electricity but now, even one glowing streetlight can confuse the little ones. Instead of scrambling toward the ocean, they may head the wrong way and end up stranded in a parking lot.

POST ⊕ FL 95 373

In a state swimming in history, Amelia Island at Exit 373 may take first prize.

French Huguenots, pirates, conquistadores, Spanish missionaries, military officers, English colonists, Confederates and even musketeers led by a Scottish soldier of fortune, have all laid claim to the wisp of land called Amelia Island.

Only 13 miles long and 4 miles wide, it has been coveted and fought over for about 450 years. Because of this unique history, eight flags have flown over Amelia Island, the only place in the United States that can make that claim. That doesn't even account for the indigenous Timuacan Indians who were the first known inhabitants.

Human inhabitants, that is.

During all the conflict and turmoil, sea turtles maintained their annual migration to the shores of the island. It's not an unusual occurrence in Florida: up to 84,000 turtles nest along its shores and these days Amelia hosts around 150 on a good year. Nevertheless — leatherbacks, loggerheads and green turtles outlasted all those who sought to conquer the island. True, now they get a hand from the Amelia Island Sea Turtle Watch, Inc. for protection from developers.

Shrimp are not so lucky.

Amelia Island's town of Fernandina Beach, also known as the **Shrimp Capital**, celebrates its outstanding history with The Isle of Eight Flags Shrimp Festival every May.

They earn bragging rights by bringing in two million pounds of Atlantic white shrimp annually.

353 🛡FL 95🛡 MILE

JAX

From the bridge near MP 353, you get a good view of downtown Jacksonville where one of America's greatest disasters occurred.

Jacksonville's Great Fire of 1901 was the largest metropolitan fire in the American South. The fire began on May 3, 1901 with a spark from a kitchen fire. It ignited piles of drying Spanish moss at a nearby mattress factory. The fire soon engulfed the downtown area.

Smoke could be seen as far north as Savannah, Georgia.

By the end of the day, 2,368 buildings were destroyed, 10,000 people were homeless and seven residents were dead. In all, 146 city blocks were destroyed.

The Confederate Monument in Hemming Park, not far from the tallest skyscraper seen from the I-95 bridge, was one of the few city landmarks to survive the fire.

POST 345

New York City was home to the silent movie industry in the early 1900's but when the moguls sought a more pleasant climate, Jacksonville became their winter home, earning it the nickname "Winter Film Capital of the World".

For twenty years, Jacksonville's film industry flourished.

Oliver Hardy (of Laurel and Hardy fame) came here too, looking for work in the blossoming film industry. In fact, Hardy's first movie, Outwitting Daddy, was filmed in Jacksonville. It was the first of 50 one-reel films made here at the Lubin Studio.

This still from Lucky Dog features Hardy (in the middle) but was not filmed in Jacksonville.

More than good advertising!

That giant 62-feet tall 7-Up can near MP 345 is a water tower in disguise.

Over 325,000 gallons of water circulate through the "can" each day as part of the production of 7-Up, A&W Rootbeer, Hawaiian Punch and more.

The sign at Exit 318 reminds travelers that
St. Augustine is the nation's oldest city.

September 8th is the anniversary of Pedro Menendez de
Aviles' arriving on this spit of land in 1565.

The town of St. Augustine grew despite hurricanes, pirates, war
and sickness making it the oldest continuously occupied city in
the US that was founded by a European.

Town fathers don't take that distinction lightly; an annual
celebration, which grows larger each year, pays tribute to all
who had a hand in the success of the city. That includes the
indigenous Timucuan Indians who, the city's web site points out,
broke bread with the Europeans well before turkey was offered
in Plymouth, Massachusetts.

They've been wrasslin' gators at this location since 1920.

The St. Augustine Alligator Farm began as a kitschy sideshow to
lure tourists to a museum but grew into a more sophisticated jaw-
dropping attraction. The entry fee has evolved as well. For $21.95
visitors are wowed by all of the world's 23 species of crocodilians.

POST 296

The overpass near MP 296 looks terribly overgrown with weeds and that's on purpose. Constructed by the Florida Department of Transportation, its sole purpose is (and always was) an animal foot bridge, or rather a hoof and paw bridge.

Old King's Road near MP 296 echoes the area's long history.

Timucuan Indians first blazed the path to connect their villages.

The Spanish conquistadores used the route for over two hundred years.

The British got to work in the 1760's turning it into the 16-foot-wide stage coach route called King's Road.

During the second Spanish occupation, the road wasn't used much so when Americans took over in 1821, they had to rebuild the road. Even today, a trip along King's Road often looks like it did in those early days with swampy undergrowth and tangled trees decorated with Spanish moss.

278 MILE

Extravagant plantations speckled this area in the 1800's. Adventurous entrepreneurs endured the heat, mosquitoes and angry Indians to build fortunes growing indigo, rice and even potatoes.

The highlight of Flagler County's official seal is a potato. Perhaps, not for long. The potato, which once represented the lifeblood of the area, was chosen as its most important symbol when the county was officially organized in 1917. Today's councilmen are digging for a new look.

One of the most successful was Bulow Plantation, less than two miles east of the interstate at MP 280. Its story has an unusual twist.

Major Charles Wilhelm Bulow died soon after establishing the antebellum plantation in 1821. The whole lot transferred to his son, John Bulow, who successfully increased production of sugar cane (shown here), rice, cotton and indigo.

But he was known as a wild character.

He cultivated friends as easily as crops and was known for throwing great parties. In fact, according to the Southern History web site, the property's boat dock is built on broken liquor bottles.

Young Bulow was a friend to the Seminoles at a time when the government was trying to rid Florida of Indians. In the end, it was the Seminoles who burned Bulow Plantation. Today, all that stands at Bulow Ruins Historic State Park are a few ruins of what was once one of the grandest and most productive plantations in Florida.

POST FL 95 268

Daytona gets the glory but auto racing got its start on Ormond Beach, the "Birthplace of Speed."

Soon after the turn of the 19th century, auto enthusiasts found Ormond Beach's smooth, hard beaches ideal for letting loose – something not easily done on the washboard roads on dry land.

By 1902, innovators like Henry Ford, Louis Chevrolet and Ransom Olds (shown here) were driving their toys, uh – cars, along these beaches but competitive racing began in earnest a year later.

Slow pokes, they were not. Fred Marriott achieved a top speed of 127 mph in 1906 driving the Stanley Steamer, shattering the Land Speed Record worldwide.

Racing action eventually moved to Daytona, of course. The fastest average time recorded at the Daytona 500 was 177 mph set in 1980; a record that stands today.

You don't know Florida unless you know about Henry Flagler.

Roads, schools and towns are named for the man who is credited with transforming Florida from a swampy no-man's-land into a profitable tourist destination. Here, it's Flagler County.

He did it by building a few destination hotels then bringing northerners in on a newly-constructed railroad.

Without Flagler, there would not be Miami or Palm Beach.

Daytona Speedway

You are more likely to hear the Daytona Speedway than see it. Although it is less than a mile away from the interstate (directly east just north of Exit 261) the underbrush prevents any kind of a view.

Since it hosted the first Daytona 500 in 1959, it has grown to be NASCAR's premier showcase. In February, fans descend on Daytona from all over the world to see America's most prestigious car race. Indy 500 fans might quibble about that title, but around here there is no doubt about it.

Ponce Inlet Lighthouse

This striking lighthouse has stood in the Ponce de Leon Inlet since 1887. When it was first erected, however, the area was called Mosquito Inlet – more descriptive but less inviting than the current name.

Ponce de Leon, the Spanish explorer and contemporary of Christopher Columbus, was the first Spaniard to visit the peninsula. He left his mark, naming the area "florida" for the many flowers. Since accurate records of his voyages do not exist, it's unclear exactly where Ponce de Leon first made landfall. Some say it was here at the inlet that now bears his name.

POST 256

Gamble Place

In such close proximity to Disney World, it's worth mentioning that the Gamble family (of Procter and Gamble fame) dabbled in a fanciful project of their own.

Inspired by Disney's 1937 full-length movie *Snow White and the Seven Dwarves,* they built a replica of the dwarves's cottage, which is located only 1.5 miles from I-95 in the woods around Port Orange near MP 256.

DAYTONA BEACH

The town is not shy about self-promotion, as this elaborate interstate sign clearly shows. But why should they be?

There is a lot to boast about. Not only do they have the speedway and the famous beach where cars are allowed, but the Ladies Professional Golf Association (LPGA) is headquartered here.

MERRITT ISLAND

On the same island where NASA launches space ships, Merritt Island National Wildlife Refuge harbors a menagerie of animals.

The usual array of Florida critters are present but there are so many feral hogs on the island that the 140,000-acre refuge issues feral hog hunting licenses to residents.

The dictionary definition of a feral animal is one which has escaped from a domestic or captive status and is living more or less as a wild animal.

So many people travel to Florida to escape the winter cold but Florida is certainly not immune to drastic weather. Douglas Dummett found that out firsthand.

The Dummett family was already established in the sugar cane industry when the son, Douglas, bought up some land on Merritt Island to try his hand at growing citrus. A true entrepreneur, he played with grafting the tops of sweet oranges onto the base of heartier sour orange trees and, voila, started a budding business in Indian River citrus. Not only did he grow it himself but he sold the grafted rootstock to other plantation owners.

Dummett's trees survived Merritt Island's 1835 freeze.

They survived the Second Seminole War (1835-1842); unlike his peers, Douglas Dummett did not abandon his fields during the conflict.

They survived Dummett's death in 1873.

But a savage hurricane in 1893, followed the next year by a devastating freeze, wiped out his crop. If it wasn't for those saplings sold to other farmers, we wouldn't have those luscious Indian River citrus (which are primarily grown farther south).

Hurricanes and sudden freezes come to the Florida coast once in a blue moon but thunderstorms are another matter altogether.

Unlike their northern counterparts, Florida thunderstorms are usually concentrated in a small area, generally no more than 15 miles in diameter.

Their power, however, comes from a "stacking effect" – the thunderheads grow upwards, sometimes 10 miles into the atmosphere.

The result is powerful, pelting rain that lasts a short time. The record rainfall around Merritt Island was almost 12 inches of rain in one hour.

Originally called Cape Canaveral by Spanish explorers, the name means "place of cane or reeds," like those shown above.

President Truman launched test missiles from the cape as early as 1949.

President Eisenhower established NASA in 1958 with a mission to "pioneer the future in space exploration, scientific discovery and aeronautics research."

But it was President John Kennedy who put it on the map by issuing a challenge in 1961: "landing a man on the Moon and returning him back safely to the earth."

This was achieved when Apollo 11 blasted off from here then returned to earth with the first astronauts to walk on the moon.

The year was 1969, six years after Kennedy's assassination.

Renaming the area Cape Kennedy after the president's assassination was so unpopular that it was changed back to Cape Canaveral. The Launch Operations Center, however, was changed to Kennedy Space Center seven days after his death.

That name stuck.

POST FL 95 215

MOONSTONE: THE STATE GEM

It's not naturally found in Florida. It's not found on the moon. But the moonstone, a shimmery, whitish feldspar, was designated Florida's official gem in 1970 to memorialize Apollo 11's historic trip to the moon.

Ancient Romans admired the gem too; they thought it might have been made from drops of moonlight.

The American Police Hall of Fame and Museum is not far from Exit 215.

This is the first museum dedicated to police who died in the line of duty. Much more than a memorial, visitors get a peek into the on-duty lives of police. What other museum has a shooting range?

WINDOVER SITE
An ancient burial site found a half mile from I-95 just south of Exit 215.

Imagine this: a backhoe digger, hired to clean out an unused swampy bog, caught a glimpse of something strange in a scoop of peat. It was a human skull.

Police were brought in and, after further investigation, skeletons of 168 people were found in the bog. They wondered, "Could it be a mass murder?".

Scientists determined that it was a mass grave from the Early Archaic Period (6,000 - 5,000 BC) and one of archeology's most amazing finds. After 7,000 years, brain tissue was still moist and stomach contents were rather "fresh." The most endearing scene was surely the three-year old whose body, still wrapped in a fabric shroud, was found cradling a beloved toy.

MELBOURNE

Melbourne's first postmaster lived in Melbourne, Australia for a while. He had the privilege of naming the town.

This view of botanical gardens in Melbourne, Australia illustrates some of the areas' similarities and part of the reason the postmaster chose the name.

A <u>MAMMOTH</u>? YES! This might not be the place you'd expect to find evidence of prehistoric animals but this mammoth skeleton (fleshed out for display) was unearthed here in Melbourne.

And he wasn't alone: further excavation uprooted bones of camels, mastodons, saber tooth cats and much more.

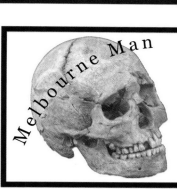

Melbourne Man

They found more than wild animals here; the skeleton of a seven-foot tall human was also unearthed. Melbourne Man, as scientists call him, lived about 10,000 years ago, meaning he coexisted with (and probably hunted) the mammoth and its peers.

Another noteworthy man lived around here.

Fans from all over the world travel to an out-of-the-way cemetery in Paris to pay respects to the simple grave of **Jim Morrison** of The Doors.

You, without even trying, will zip past the place of his birth — Melbourne, Florida.

If you are driving the entire length of Florida, you've reached the halfway point. Melbourne is about midway between Jacksonville and Miami.

Near MP 161, I-95 crosses over the impressive Canal 54.

At top highway speed, you won't see its most famous visitor but from November to March, manatees tend to gather in the canal, looking for a warm place to eat lunch.

Christopher Columbus was the first European to report seeing this slug-like mammal who slightly resembles its closest relative, the elephant.

The manatees share the canal with the Florida Tech rowing team. The calm long waterway is ideal for practice.

Another visitor to the area is the armadillo, "the little armored one."

Usually associated with Texas and neighboring states, it's common to run across an armadillo in this area.

POST 156

Spanish galleons, heavy with gold, silver and gems from Mexico, often plied the waters off the Florida coast on the way back to Spain.

That was the plan of the 11 (some say 12) Spanish treasures ships that set out for home in 1715.

A nasty hurricane caught up to them, though, and scuttled all but one ship.

It happened right here at Exit 156, at the location of today's Sebastian River Preserve State Park. At the time, Spanish governors sent salvage crews to the scene partly to help the 1000 survivors but mostly to gather up the valuable goods.

They didn't get it all – not a long shot.

Even today, especially after a heavy storm that churns the seas, a coin from the Spanish galleons might surface on the beach.

The McLarty Treasure Museum in the Sebastian Inlet State Park displays some of the found treasure.

Travelers on the road to escape winter's cold might like to know that at Exit 147 they have finally reached the

"Gateway to the Tropics."

Northern Vero Beach is subtropical while southern Vero Beach basks in a tropical climate. This unusual distinction results in an extravagance of vegetation. Just look along the side of the interstate: oak trees mingle with palmettos; pine trees coexist with grapefruit trees.

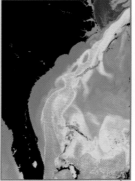

The Gulf Stream has something to do with the area's temperate climate. Take a look at a map of Florida. Vero Beach is about 100 miles farther east than Jacksonville. It juts out into that warm Gulf Stream current shown here in orange. Cooler water appears green in this satellite image.

Because the temperature is more reliably frost-free (although there is still the rogue cold snap), Vero Beach is also called the "Citrus Capital of the World."

Have you ever tasted **sweet Indian River Grapefruit** during the dreary winter months? As you can see by the groves near MP 137, this is where it comes from.

The area's soil, calcium-rich Anastasia limestone, is particularly suited to growing citrus.

There's more to their citrus success story, however.

When the thermometer dips below freezing, area farmers have a secret weapon. The land is so uniformly flat that, when inclement weather is forecast, farmer's can flood the fields with water, which acts like a blanket. It boosts temperatures 2 to 4 degrees, enough to save the crops.

The Indian River District grows 70% of Florida's grapefruit crop. Much of it is shipped to Japan; in fact, 95% of citrus that goes to Japan comes from this area.

"You are just like a Florida Cracker!"

Is it a compliment? Is it an insult? Both, it seems – depending on who you're talking to. It's hard to pin down since the definition itself is debatable.

- Some might say it refers to a native Floridian. But that's not quite right. Those who grew up under the glittering lights of Miami would not qualify.

- Others believe it is tied to Florida's long tradition of raising cattle. But that, too, is fraught with controversy. No one knows for sure how Florida cowboys got the name Crackers, but one likely explanation is the crack made by their whips, which they used instead of lassos like their Spanish counterparts.

- Some say it refers to someone, native or not, who has the spirit of self-reliance. There, that might be the closest to the character of a Florida Cracker.

Whatever the historical explanation is (and after years of dickering, the mystery is never likely to be solved), some people proudly refer to themselves as Crackers and others, well, just don't mention it. Riders in the Florida Cracker Trail, an annual cross state trail ride that ends in Fort Pierce at Exit 131, wear the name with pride. The stated purpose of the 120-mile ride is to draw attention to Florida's horse and cattle heritage.

Lake Okeechobee, about 25 west of the interstate via either Exit 101 or 87, is second only to Lake Michigan as the largest freshwater lake contained completely within the continental US.
The "Big O," as it's called, is above sea level and held in place with a 20-foot high dike.

You Are Here

Lake Okeechobee

The Loxahatchee River, which means river of turtles in the Seminole language, sneaks beneath I-95 unnoticed, cloaked in trees and bushes, about two miles north of Exit 87. From there it meanders east past Trapper Nelson's homestead.

These turtles basking along a Florida river probably don't care but the Loxahatchee was the first river designated as a "Wild and Scenic River" by the federal government. That means it and about 150 similar rivers are protected from development to preserve their unique scenic beauty.

ROLL CAMERAS!

The story of Vincent Natulkiewicz reads like a Hollywood script.
Near MP 90, gaze east toward the dense underbrush, the scene of a real life
thriller. It all happened about one mile from I-95.

- A young New Jersey man, in love only with nature and self-reliance, buys a remote tract of land inland near Jupiter, Florida and sets about living off the land, trapping game for survival.
- His infrequent trips to town stir up rumors and curiosity among the city folk who call him the Trapper.
- Although his cabin was (and still is) accessible only by boat, inquisitive people sometimes showed up at his doorstep.
- "Ah," he thought, "why not make a little money from this situation?" He adopted a new name (Trapper Natulkiewicz didn't quite fit his new image), and from then on, Trapper Nelson was considered the real life Tarzan of the Loxahatchee River.
- At 6'4", his physic matched the role.
- His shows (alligator wrestling, snake handling) and zoo attracted plenty of tourists to the jungle oasis, including famous ones like Gary Cooper and rich ones like local heiresses.
- The end to the story came in 1968 in a similarly dramatic fashion; Trapper Nelson's friend found him at home with a bullet in his head.
- Although an investigation was inconclusive, it was probably a suicide.

His homestead, now located within the Jonathan Dickinson State Park, was preserved. Tours are available through the park service.

59 🛡FL 95 MILE

Rosemary Scrub Natural Area

Rarely can it be claimed that the construction of an interstate highway saved a natural area from development. But it happened near MP 59.

This example of Florida Scrub is in the Ocala National Forest.

On the west side of the road, enclosed with chain link fencing, is the Rosemary Scrub Natural Area.

This 14-acre strip of land wedged between a housing plan and railroad tracks doesn't look like much but it's an ecological oasis.

It's there because the interstate severed an access road where a strip mall had been proposed. Without access, the plot of land became useless to developers. Still, it cost nearly a half million dollars for the county and city to purchase the land, which they preserved in its natural state – much like the barefoot mailmen would have encountered a hundred years ago.

One resident that isn't bothered by the fence is the Florida Scrub Jay. Found only in Florida, it swoops in to gather acorns dropped from the oak trees or to search for caterpillars and small lizards. As Florida Scrub loses ground to development, the Florida Scrub Jay loses its habitat – the scrub is the only place the jay calls home.

JOB OPENING: BAREFOOT MAILMAN
Perfect for the sports-minded outdoorsy type.

Ed Hamilton, a Kentucky fellow who moved to Florida in the late 1800's to dabble in the citrus business, applied for a job with the post office. Although Florida was mostly wilderness and roads were practically nonexistent, the state was developing and the mail had to get through. Before 1885, delivery of a letter sent from Palm Beach to Miami could take two months. Most of the trip was by steamer and traveled to New York City, then to Cuba, before getting to Miami, about 68 miles away.

That's when someone thought up the job of a long-distance pedestrian mailman. Walking from here to Miami and back, the trip took one week.

Ed's $600 a year job was this: every Monday he'd leave Palm Beach heading south with a mailbag and everything he needed for the week secured in a black oilcloth satchel. He walked (barefoot of course) along the sand until he came to an inlet where a rowboat was strategically tied. Alternately walking and rowing, he completed the 68-mile trip, delivered the mail then turned around and headed back to Palm Beach. The system ran like clockwork until one day Ed didn't make it to Miami. A search party found his mailbag, personal belongings and clothes on the sand at the edge of an inlet but the boat was tied on the opposite shore. Oh yes, there were plenty of alligator tracks too.

No one knows exactly what happened but a good guess is that someone "borrowed" the boat and tied it to the wrong shore. When Ed went to retrieve it, he met his end.

Barefoot Mailman Day is still recognized in Palm Beach with an annual celebration that includes a partial recreation of Ed's route, alligator chili and a Spanish doubloon hunt.

His story is told at the Palm Beach County Museum.

RAINBOW INTERCHANGE NEAR MP 25

Called the Rainbow Interchange for obvious reasons, this is part of an I-95 segment that carries 300,000 per day. It's the busiest stretch of highway in Florida - but not the busiest intersection.

The Golden Glades Interchange in Miami (where I-95, the Turnpike, three state roads, some side streets and a rail line converge) is crowned the busiest intersection in the state.
That's at Exit 12. But this one is prettier.

The Ft. Lauderdale Hollywood International Airport has grown from a small airfield to Broward County's largest employer but it grew in a congested area.

Now it coexists with thousands of homeowners with sensitive ears.

Ten noise monitors continuously measure decibels of the nearly 1,000 daily flights passing through facility at MP 24.

Airplanes taking off are noisier than those that are landing. But, says the airport's web site, incoming planes fly lower longer so the noise impact is about the same.

POST 20

BOOMERS ON DANIA BEACH

Locals say it's a great place to go if you are all beached out.

Coaster fans can get their fix any day of the week since Boomers swings its doors open every single day to welcome fun seekers.

Boomers' web site claims that the roller coaster shown here is the only one in Southern Florida. But, of course, there's more than that. Bumper boats, bowling, batting cages – they have it all.

Hollywood and the Seminoles (MP 20)

The diverse Indian tribes found throughout Florida were conveniently lumped together and called Seminoles in the 1770's. The name meant "wild people" or "runaway." Florida Seminoles refer to themselves as the "Unconquered People" and for good reason. The United States government waged three wars against the Seminoles, trying to either eradicate them or move them to Oklahoma. They nearly succeeded. It is estimated that about 300 Indians escaped into Florida swamps after the third Seminole War. They laid low for decades, gathering strength, until trading posts around Ft. Lauderdale, Chokoloskee and other places lured them out of the wilds. That was in the late 19th century. Since then, the Seminoles have flourished. Now about 3,000 Seminoles live on six reservations throughout the state, most notably in the Hollywood area where they opened the first Native American high stakes casino in 1979.

Osceola, shown here, was a Seminole leader who was tricked into surrendering.

The "modern" town began here. Miami was incorporated in one of these wooden buildings.

Miami means "big water" in the native Calusa language.

Searching for a potion to get a darker tan, Miami Beach pharmacist Benjamin Green literally cooked up a concoction based on cocoa butter in 1944. He invented the first suntan cream, which eventually took the name **Coppertone**.

Take Exit 3 to get to Port Miami. If that's your destination, you join well over four million other fun-seekers who board annually at the "Cruise Capital of the World." For over 20 years, Miami has held the title as the number one cruising port.

THE ANCIENT, MYSTERIOUS MIAMI CIRCLE

You'd think $8.5 million would buy the right to build whatever and whenever you wanted but that's not necessarily so. A Miami property developer paid that amount for a site in the city, tore down the existing building with the intention of erecting a new high-rise. But a routine archeological survey found evidence of what is believed to be a 1,900-year-old Tequesta Indian village. All further construction was stopped.

Called the Miami Circle, it consists of 24 large holes carved into the bedrock to form a circle 38 feet in diameter. Many artifacts were found in the indentations; shell tools, human teeth and stone axe heads to name a few. What may be the oldest permanent settlement in the US, this Tequesta village was extensive. In fact, the Miami Hilton and Miami Convention Center, both just across the street, are no doubt built on additional remains of the important site.

Near MP 2, look east toward the skyscrapers of downtown Miami. That's where the ancient site overshadows all the modern construction. The view also illustrates why Miami is called the "Manhattan of the South." Those buildings represent the largest concentration of international banks in the US.

THE END

This is not the southernmost interstate mile in the United States interstate system. That's in Hawaii.
But in the continental US, at this point you are officially as far south as you can go on the interstate.

VISITORS INFORMATION
TO SELECTED SITES AND HIGHLIGHTED TOWNS

Every effort was made to give you accurate and timely facts. If you choose to visit a place, please contact them for up-to-the-minute admission charges and hours of operation.

Basic contact information is provided here to help you search for further information about a site or topic.

A couple of things you should know about the entries in this book:
- While the sites mentioned may be fascinating and worth a stop, an appearance here is not an endorsement.
- Every entry was chosen simply for its entertainment value; that is, nobody paid to be in the book.

6	Houlton, ME	www.houlton-maine.com/
7	Smyrna, ME	www.aroostook.me.us/smyrna/
8	Aroostook County	www.visitaroostook.com/
10	Millinocket, ME	www.millinocket.org/
11	Katahdin	www.mtkatahdin.com/
14	Old Town, ME	www.old-town.lib.me.us/
15	Bangor, ME	www.bangorcvb.org/
19	Skowhegan, ME	www.skowhegan.org/
20	Augusta, ME	www.augustamaine.gov/
	Popham Colony	http://mfship.org
21	Old Fort Western	www.oldfortwestern.org/
	207-626-2385	
	16 Cony St.	
24	Old Orchard Beach, ME	www.oldorchardbeachmaine.com/
	Palace Playland	www.palaceplayland.com/
	207-934-2414	
	1 Old Orchard St.	
	Old Orchard Beach, ME	
25	The Kennebunks, ME	www.visitthekennebunks.com/
26	Kittery, ME	www.visitmaine.net/kittery
	Fort McClary	www.fortmcclary.org/
	207-384-5160	
	Kittery Point	

Call for current hours of operation and admission charges.

VISITORS INFORMATION
TO SELECTED SITES AND HIGHLIGHTED TOWNS

27 Portsmouth, NH www.portsmouthnh.com/

Portsmouth Naval Shipyard
757-393-8591
2 High Street

33 Newburyport, MA www.newburyportchamber.org/

Custom House Maritime Museum
978-462-8681
25 Water St.

34 Salem, MA www.salemweb.com/

36 Minuteman National Historic Park
www.nps.gov/mima/index.

37 Concord, MA www.newenglandtravelplanner.com/

Concord Museum www.concordmuseum.org/
978-369-9763
200 Lexington Road

37 Orchard House www.louisamayalcott.org/
978-369-4118
399 Lexington Road

39 Plymouth, MA www.visit-plymouth.com/

41 Providence, RI www.goprovidence.com/

42 International Scholar Athlete Hall of Fame
1-800-447-9889 www.internationalsport.com/
3045 Kingstown Road
Kingston, RI

46 Mystic, CT www.mysticchamber.org/

Mystic Seaport www.mysticseaport.org/
860-572-5315
75 Greenmanville Avenue

48 Florence Griswold Museum
860-434-5542 www.flogris.org/
96 Lyme Street, Old Lyme, CT

49 Old Saybrook, CT www.oldsaybrookchamber.com/

51 New Haven, CT www.cityofnewhaven.com/

Louis' Lunch http://louislunch.com/
203-562-5507
261-263 Crown St.

52 Bridgeport, CT www.greater-bridgeport.com/

P.T. Barnum Museum www.barnum-museum.org/
203-331-1104
820 Main Street

Call for current hours of operation and admission charges.

53 **Birdcraft Sactuary** www.ctaudubon.org/visit/birdcraft
203-259-0416
314 Unquowa Road, Fairfield, CT

54 **Norwalk, CT** www.norwalkct.org/

Lockwood-Mathews Mansion
203-838-9799 www.lockwoodmathewsmansion.com/
295 West Avenue, Norwalk, CT

62 **Bordentown, NJ** www.downtownbordentown.com/

65 **Haddonfield, NJ** www.haddonfieldnj.org/

70 **Philadelphia, PA** www.visitphilly.com/

Elfreth's Alley Assc. www.elfrethsalley.org/
215-574-0560
126 Elfreth's Alley

71 **Christ Church** www.christchurchphila.org/
2nd Street above Market

73 **Heinz Wildlife Refuge** www.friendsoftinicummarsh.org/

74 **Frawley Stadium** www.bluerocks.com/

75 **Wilmington, DE** www.visitwilmingtonde.com/

79 **Havre de Grace, MD** www.hdgtourism.com/

Decoy Museum www.decoymuseum.com
410-939-3739
215 Giles St.

80 **Tudor Hall** http://juniusbooth.org/
(Center for the Arts)
410-838-2177
17 Tudor Lane, Bel Air, MD

84 **The White House** www.whitehouse.gov/

86 **Washington DC** http://washington.org/

88 **Alexandria, VA** www.visitalexandriava.com/

89 **Contraband and Freedmens Cemetery** www3.alexandriava.gov/freedmens/

90 **Weems-Botts Museum** www.historicdumfries.com/weemsbotts
703-221-2218
3944 Cameron St., Dumfries, VA

91 **Quantico Marine Base** www.quantico.usmc.mil/
703-630-0488

91 **National Museum of the Marine Corps** www.usmcmuseum.com/
1-877-635-1775
18900 Jefferson Davis Hwy, Triangle, VA

Call for current hours of operation and admission charges.

VISITORS INFORMATION
TO SELECTED SITES AND HIGHLIGHTED TOWNS

92 **Spotsylvania, VA**   www.spotsylvania.org/

    Battle of Chancellorsville www.nps.gov/frsp/

93 **Civil War Life Museum**   www.civilwar-life.com
    540-834-1859
    4712 Southpoint Pkwy.
    Fredericksburg, VA

95 **Kings Dominion**_____   www.kingsdominion.com/

96 **Richmnd**   www.visitrichmondva.com

    **Museum of the Confederacy at the Confederate
    White House**   www.moc.org/
    804-649-1861
    1201 E. Clay St.

97 **Museum of Edgar Allan Poe**
    804-648-5523   www.poemuseum.org/
    1914-16 East Main St.

    Lumpkins Jail
    The eastern end of E. Franklin Rd.
    Other markers of the slave auction era:
    www.hmdb.org/marker.asp?marker=20779

    Triple Crossing
    www.hmdb.org/marker.asp?marker=23912

101 **Petersburg, VA**   www.petersburgarea.org/

    Petersburg National Battlefield
                www.nps.gov/pogr
    804-458-9504 – Grant's Headquarters

106 **Roanke, VA**   www.visitroanokeva.com/

109 **Inner Banks**   www.ibxlifestyles.com/

110 **Wilson, NC**   www.wilson-nc.com/

111 **Tobacco Farm**   www.tobaccofarmlifemuseum.org/
    Life Museum
    919-284-3431
    709 Church St, Kenly, NC

112 **Selma, NC**   http://johnstoncountync.org/

    Ruby Theater   www.amjubilee.com
    919-202-9927
    300 Raiford St. Selma, NC

113 **Eva Gardner Museum**   www.avagardner.org/
    919-934-5830
    325 E. Market St, Smithfield, NC

    Historic Union Station www.visitnc.com/listings/view/50868

114 **Benson**   www.townofbenson.com

Call for current hours of operation and admission charges.

VISITORS INFORMATION
TO SELECTED SITES AND HIGHLIGHTED TOWNS

115 Spivey's Corner and the www.hollerincontest.com/
Hollerin' Contest
910-567-2600

116 Fort Bragg Museum www.asomf.org/
910-643-2766
100 Bragg Blvd., Fayetteville, NC

123 South of the Border www.thesouthoftheborder.com/

125 Darlington Raceway www.darlingtonraceway.com/

126 Sumter, SC www.sumtersc.gov/visitingus/tourism.

127 Swan Lake Iris Gardens
803-436-2640
822 W. Liberty St. Sumter, SC

128 Manning www.cityofmanning.org/

129 Lake Marion www.sciway.net/city/lake-marion-sc.

130 Charleston, SC www.charleston.com/

132 Walterboro, SC www.walterborosc.org/

135 Harold's Country Club
843-589-4360
Yemassee, SC

140 SAM Shortline http://samshortline.com/

141 Mighty Eighth Air Force Museum
912-748-8888 www.mightyeighth.org/
175 Bourne Ave. Pooler, GA

142 Savannah, GA www.savannahvisit.com/

143 Richmond Hill, GA http://richmondhillcvb.org/

145 Historic Liberty Trail
www.discoverlibertyga.com/libertytrail.asp

Geechee Kunda Cultural Arts Center
912-884-4440
622 Ways Temple Rd. Riceboro, GA

146 Fort King George
www.gastateparks.org/FortKingGeorge
912-437-4770

148 Brunswick, GA www.brunswickgeorgia.net/

150 Woodbine, GA http://woodbinegeorgia.net/

Woodbine Opry www.woodbineopry.com/
912-264-8019
Corner of 2nd Ave. & Camden Ave.

151 St. Marys, GA www.stmaryswelcome.com/

155 Amelia Island, FL www.ameliaisland.com/

Call for current hours of operation and admission charges.

VISITORS INFORMATION
TO SELECTED SITES AND HIGHLIGHTED TOWNS

156 Jacksonville, FL www.visitjacksonville.com/

158 St. Augustine, FL www.oldcity.com/

St. Augustine Alligator Farm
904-824-3337 www.alligatorfarm.com/
999 Anastasia Blvd, St.

160 Bulow Ruins Historic State Park
www.floridastateparks.org/bulowplantation/
386-517-2084
County Rd 2001, Flagler Beach, FL

162 Daytona www.daytonabeach.com/

Daytona Speedway
www.daytonainternationalspeedway.com/

162 Ponce Inlet Lighthouse www.ponceinlet.org/
386-761-1821
4931 S. Peninsula Dr. Ponce Inlet, FL

163 Gamble Place www.moas.org/gambleplace
386-255-3015
1819 Taylor Rd, Port Orange, FL

164 Merritt Island Natl. Wildlife Refuge
www.fws.gov/merrittisland/

166 NASA www.nasa.gov/

167 American Police Hall of Fame www.aphf.org/museummap.pdf
321-264-0911
6350 Horizon Dr. Titusville, FL

171 McLarty Treasure Museum www.atocha1622.com/mclarty.htm
772-589-2147
13180 North A1A, Vero Beach, FL

172 Vero Beach, FL www.verobeach.com/

175 Jonathan Dickinson State Park
www.floridastateparks.org/jonathandickinson/
561-746-1466
16450 SE Federal Hwy, Hobe Sound, FL

177 Palm Beach, FL www.palmbeachfl.com/

Palm Beach County Museum www.pbchistoryonline.org
561-832-4164
300 N. Dixie Highway

178 Ft. Lauderdale, FL www.sunny.org/visitors/

179 Hollywood, FL www.visithollywoodfl.org/

Boomers www.boomersparks.com/

180 Miami, FL www.hellomiami.com

181 Miami Circle www.flheritage.com/archaeology/projects/

Call for current hours of operation and admission charges.

IMAGE CREDITS

MAINE TO FLORIDA

www.interestinginterstates.com

QUICK ORDER FORM
Any purchase may be returned for a full refund minus S&H.

DESCRIPTION	QTY.	UNIT PRICE	TOTAL
What's Great About I-95: Maine to Florida		$22.95	
Shipping & Handling			
Add Sales Tax for PA deliveries		6% PA 7% Philly & Pgh	
		TOTAL	

Shipping & Handling:
U.S. Deliveries - Please add $5.00 for the first
book and $2.00 for each additional book.

If sending to multiple locations include the Shipping & Handling Charge
for each destination. List additional destinations on a separate sheet.

By phone:	☎ 412-487-7177
Online:	💻 www.interestinginterstates.com
By mail	📧 Send this form along with your check to:

Barbara Barnes
Opal Publishing Company
2167 Ferguson Road
Allison Park, PA 15101

Send To:

Name:

Address:

City: ST: Zip:

Phone:

Email: